What's Next
For You?

FERNANDO L. SOTO

Published by Fate Publishing, LLC.
www.fatepublishsing.com

Books may be purchased in quantity and/or special sales by contacting the publisher at 888-317-8374 or support@fatepublishing.com. Copyright © 2013 Fernando L. Soto
All rights reserved.

ISBN: 0615943764
ISBN-13: 9780615943763

First Edition, 2012
No part of this book may be reproduced or transmitted in any form or by any means, electronic or mechanical, including photocopying, recording or by any information storage and retrieval system, without written permission from the author and / or publisher, except for the inclusion of brief quotations.

Author Photography: www.spiercephotography.com
Senior Editor: Melissa Gough New York, New York

Readers should be aware that Internet Web sites offered as citations and / or sources for further information may have changed or disappeared between the time this book was written and when it was read.

This book is the work of the author's experience and opinion and it was written to educate and entertain. The author and publisher shall have neither liability nor responsibility to any person or entity with respect to any loss or damage caused, or alleged to have been caused, directly or indirectly, by the information contained in this book.

This book is dedicated to the four most important women in my life- My Mom Edna, my wife Alfa and my two beautiful daughters, Thalia and Edni. Anything is possible.

ACKNOWLEDGEMENTS

Books are written in many ways. This one is the result of many failures, challenges and successes I have experienced in my life. It is the collective mistakes and wisdom gained from many of the things I have done and many of the people that I know: My family, friends, coworkers, employers, customers and employees. It is also the pages of insight I gained from reading others who have succeeded and gone on to share their personal educations, too. We all have the opportunity to benefit from what others have written about achieving our goals and living the life we all dream of living.

The acknowledgement of individual people would not do justice to everyone who has contributed to my life, and thus to this book. I know that I would forget to name someone. So I am officially acknowledging and thanking every single person in my life who has encouraged me to live my dream and write this book. You all know who you are. Now know that if it weren't for you, I would not be where I am today. I would also not be in a position to help others as you have helped me.

This book was written from the heart because it is so close to my heart and it is written for you because I know you have a dream and are searching for a way to live that dream.

Read on, my friends. I hope someday you are all in a position to thank others for helping you get to the place where you want to be in life.

TABLE OF CONTENTS

Dedication iii
Acknowledgements. v
Introduction. ix
Preface xi

PART ONE: Are You Ready to Live Your Dream?
Chapter 1: Focus is Everything 1
Chapter 2: What's Next for You? 7
Chapter 3: Why Work is So Important. 12
Chapter 4: Attitude Makes a Difference 20
Chapter 5: Never Settle. 24
Chapter 6: Inspiration and Influences. 33
Chapter 7: Are You Ready to Live Your Dream? 38

PART TWO: How to Live Your Dream
Chapter 8: The Personal Timesheet 45
Chapter 9: Change is Good 53
Chapter 10: Staying on Track 63
Chapter 11: The Daily Worksheet. 75
Chapter 12: Four Key Truths. 87
Chapter 13: Naysayers and Setbacks 95
Chapter 14: Why Persistence and Consistency Count 103

WHAT'S NEXT FOR YOU?

PART THREE: What Are You Waiting For?
Chapter 15: A Roadmap for Success............................... 111
Chapter 16: What Passion Means to Me 120
Chapter 17: The Equation for Success 127
Chapter 18: The Frequently Asked Questions Chapter............... 135

Appendix A: Cool Stuff to Read.................................. 141
Appendix B: Forms... 145
End Notes... 147

INTRODUCTION

"The future belongs to those who believe in the beauty of their dreams. You must do the things you think you cannot do."

- Eleanor Roosevelt

Although this book has a beginning and an end, Fernando's success is just beginning. He is a true example of how putting your mind to a goal can result in reaching that goal.

Do you work at a dead-end job, but feel you are destined for more? Do you have a drive or passion that you can't put a finger on? Is your passion just beyond your grasp, but you know it is there? Many of us have worked in dead-end jobs and have felt that inner yearning. Believe it or not, Fernando has his goals paced out for the rest of his life and while some of them will change as his life progresses, he has a plan.

I had the honor of reading What's Next For You? in sections before it was published. This book has motivated me to not only continue enhancing my life, but the lives of people around me.

Many people will read these pages, strive to improve their lives, and slowly fizzle out. Others will take the parts that fit, add them to their "warehouse" and grow and others will blossom from reading this book. One thing is for sure: All of us that read Fernando's words are the starfish he describes in his book. Whether the impact is life-changing or moment-changing, this book will invoke change.

This book has the power to change your life!

WHAT'S NEXT FOR YOU?

The bottom line is: Set your mind to a goal. Set your plan. Focus on what's next for you. Become who you were meant to be. Fernando's book will help you focus and reach that inner, better you.

You are almost there!

David Pasquini

PREFACE

"The mind that opens to a new idea never returns to its original size."
- Albert Einstein

Welcome.

Welcome to my life; a life where I leap from bed in the morning eager to start my day. A life where I get to hire, teach and coach people who are enthusiastic about being the best people and employees they can be. As employees of my company, they're given that opportunity. I get to live my dream life every day and I get to help my employees think about and work toward their dream lives, too.

That's what this book is all about.

If you are one of those individuals who go through life on autopilot, not really working toward what you really want to do in life, you have a choice. Dig deep into your heart and reanimate that dream you once had, or that dream you still have. You can leap from a good night's sleep and catapult yourself into a new workday that challenges you, fulfills you and energizes you. I do it and you can, too.

I started out far from where I am today. I worked hard for decades and got nowhere. I wasn't living the life that I saw for myself and pondered about all the choices I had as I lived my life. I could stay where I was, working day in and day out at something I didn't enjoy, or I could believe in myself and in the dreams I had for myself and do something about it. I was unhappy and I was at the bottom of my game. Things weren't working…and then one morning, I woke up.

I woke up and decided that I was ready to change. I read every motivational book I could get my hands on and then I discovered the work of a man named Napoleon Hill and began quoting him.

> *"Whatever the mind can conceive and believe you can achieve."*
> - NAPOLEON HILL

Napoleon Hill wrote things that changed my life. I knew if I could dream it, I could become it or do it. As I began working toward my dream of owning a business, many things took place. It was hard and scary and exciting and when I finally reached my goals, I was at the top of my game. Working toward my dream life brought me to a place I had never been. The pursuit polished me out and helped me become better at almost everything, initially, a better employee and then a better husband, a better father, relative, employer and better at managing my time. I am a better person because I am happy. I am happy because I am living my dreams. I am living my dreams because I gave my life the attention it deserved.

So welcome to your soon-to-be new life. It is my hope that by the time you finish reading this book, you'll realize that literally, anything is within your reach and that if you can think it and dream it, well…you can do it!

I do feel that I have to warn you, though. In the pages ahead, you will learn how to live your dreams, but it's not for everyone. Bringing your life to a higher standard and striving for the things that you believe in and want to accomplish in your life is hard work. You will fill out charts and write words on index cards. You will read lots of books and rent movies that inspire you. You will learn to manage your time and prioritize all the things you will need to do. You will learn to ask yourself, "What's next for me?"

It will be scary and hard and awesome all at the same time, but when it's all said and done, you will be happier and living your dream…no matter what that dream is. I did it and so can you.

PART ONE

Chapter One
FOCUS IS EVERYTHING

"Whatever the mind can conceive and believe you can achieve."[1]
— Napoleon Hill

Imagine waking up in the morning, leaping out of bed and racing out the door to go to work. You're confident and satisfied with how you spend your days. You can't wait to see what the day has in store for you. Work is more than just work, it's a place where you're valued and respected. Going to work means stepping into a world that is challenging, stimulating and rewarding. You are a valued employee or maybe you're the boss. It's what you want to do. It's where you want to be. Imagine all of those things happening every single day.

I know how that feels.

WHAT'S NEXT FOR YOU?

I own a successful business. It's a business that requires excellent communication and presentation skills. It's a business that depends on my ability to carry myself in a certain way and interact with clients on a certain level. It's a business that was built on a strong desire to change my life…and I worked tirelessly to build the skills to make that happen. Today, my business is successful and something I am proud of. It's a dream come true.

It's my dream come true.

But this hasn't always been the case. Before starting my company, I spent nine years working 12- to 14-hour shifts each day. I worked hard and found myself getting nowhere…fast. Each day I woke up and worked at a job that was not me. It wasn't what I wanted to be doing. Since, it's important to be the best you can be no matter where you are or what you are doing, I worked as hard as I could. I lived through almost a decade of endless hours and tiresome jobs. I knew this wasn't the life I wanted to live, but I was too scared to do anything about it. For a while, I was too scared to quit my job and pursue something else. How would I replace my income? What would I do for money? Those were some of the thoughts that tore me up inside as I contemplated leaving my job. I was at least getting paid for the work I was doing, but leaving my job meant living without that paycheck. I already knew what being broke felt like and I didn't want to go back there. For many years, I was in a place where I knew I didn't belong, where I knew I could be better, but being afraid to change is bleak.

Sometimes the best place to be in this world is at the bottom because there's only one way to go: Up.

I was only 21 years old, but I could see that I was already becoming someone I had zero interest in becoming. It happened both gradually and quickly at the same time…and I know that sounds impossible, but life is so short. Time is short. Without warning and almost without notice, I began to drift off course. I knew there was more for me out there, but I was too busy working too hard to do anything about it. Before I knew it, I was in a place I never imagined myself to be.

I was at the bottom of my game, but then something happened. It wasn't anything like you see in the movies, though. It wasn't like getting hit by a bus or any one specific and jarring life-changing event. It was simply just waking up one day and looking at myself in the mirror. I was unhappy with where I was headed. I was unhappy with who I'd become. It's not who I wanted to be. I completely drifted of course and lost focus in my life. I knew I had a decision to make. Did I want to accept things the way they were and live the rest of my life working long hours at one job after another? Did I want to go through this short life not being the best I could be? Or did I want to finally recognize the dream that was inside me and maybe do something about it?

Could I live my dream?

It's been said by many people in many different ways: If you hear something enough times, you remember it. If you say something over and over again, it becomes a part of you. If you see the world in a positive way, good things happen. If you focus on what you want, you can get it.

"If you focus on what you want, you can get it."

If you live it, you can become it.

With these words of wisdom in mind, I decided to dump all of my energy and thoughts into achieving my dream. I did something every day to bring me closer to what I wanted in life. With laser focus, I zeroed in on exactly what I wanted and went after it each and every single day. At that time in my life, my dream was to stop working for others and work entirely for myself.

I knew what my dream was. I wanted to start my own business. I knew it wouldn't be easy though, but I had to get going and make it happen. I didn't want to waste any more time. It was an exciting and simply terrifying decision, but I made it and knowing what your dream is… is the first step to achieving it!

So my race began. I started chasing after my dream. The first area where I started to make changes was at work.

While working long hours at my full-time job, I began to learn how to get what I wanted. I read everything I could get my hands on about business, leadership and motivation. After dropping out of high school and drifting from job to job, I now had a purpose. I didn't have a high school diploma and I had never gone to college, but I knew a thing or two about work. I knew that hard work led to consistent positive results for my employer and when the work I did was quality, my employer was more successful. I could see it. At work, I was honest and positive. I knew that each step I took could lead me to a better life. It didn't matter that I was working at a manufacturing facility. What mattered was how I worked. How I responded to stressful situations and the people I worked with. How the job I did affected my coworkers and my employers.

Any job you do will always be just a job unless you see the possibilities and spend each day being a little better than the day before. I wanted more than just a job. I wanted a career. A career is created by the contributions you make to the organization that you work for and even the smallest change in attitude is a step closer to a career, which in turn is a step closer to your dream.

What I lacked in formal education, I made up in drive. The world around me became my classroom. I learned how to live, by living. I learned how to be a better employee, by listening and working harder with a more positive attitude. I started asking more questions. With my dream driving everything I did, I became motivated and filled with purpose.

As I focused on my dreams and worked toward them, I found myself slowly becoming what I wanted to become. The hundreds of inspirational books I read made me more inspired. I started to believe in myself. I knew I could accomplish anything. That belief became a strong desire. It became a hunger that needed to be constantly fed.

That's what happens when you decide to follow your dream.

I took that first step and now my path was being created. I went from having nothing to wanting more and that desire to want more led me to actually having more. It's incredible to see the power inside yourself become a reality. Everything started falling into place. Doors opened up and job opportunities presented themselves to me. I met and surrounded myself with positive people. My head became filled with ideas and I became more focused. Every day I saw myself as an encouraging employer that offered opportunities and a successful business owner. I visualized myself as a loyal and loving husband, wonderful father and a person that gave back by helping and teaching others. Over time – and this didn't happen overnight – I became my dream. I had acquired the skills to succeed and the tools to make my dream a reality and then, I quit my job.

Really.

It was scary. Suddenly I was on my own. The butterflies I felt in my stomach were the fear and anxiety I needed to push me to action. Now I had to succeed. I had to take what I started across the finish line. The day I resigned from my job was a life-changing day. My part-time business that I had started while working my full-time job was now generating the income I needed to break free. So I went for it. I put in my letter of resignation; the letter that now hangs in my office. It's in a frame along with the name tag I wore on my uniform at the last job I held. I look at that framed letter and name tag every day and am reminded of how far I've come. No formal education and very limited resources. All I had was a dream, but that's how simple this is. If I could get to where I am now with just a dream, so can you. Anything and everything is possible as long as you know exactly what you want and will stop at nothing to get there.

And now for a few reality checks.

It's easy to start working toward something and then end up quickly drifting off and doing something else. Life tends to get in the way and put up roadblocks. It's a tough world out there. I know. The people in your life can get in the way. Your employers may try to mold you into what they need you to be. Even your husband or wife has the power to change you in small ways that can interfere with your dream. That's why your dream has to be big. It has to be so big that it becomes larger than your life.

It has to be MONUMENTAL.

That's the battery that will power your success. If you have a dream and are passionate about it, you can achieve it. I got there, and you can, too. When you make the decision to go for your dream, you make the commitment to take that burning, obsessive desire as far as it needs to go. Only then will you succeed. Your attitude will change. The people around you will treat you differently and your life will surely change.

WHAT'S NEXT FOR YOU?

It's amazing what a dream can do.

It made me a better son, husband, father and employee. It opened me up to opportunities that were closed to me before. Chasing my dream gave me energy and surrounded me with a positive outlook that people could see. Making the time to take that first step and following through will change your life. The more you put into life, the more you will get out.

Say that with me right now. Out loud, please.

The more I put into my life, the more I will get out.

Shouldn't we, at the very least, love what we do? Shouldn't we be able to showcase our strengths and be rewarded for our efforts?

Shouldn't we be living our dreams?

This is a story about how to get to where you want to go. It's about beating the odds in life and living your dreams. It's about taking your desire and learning the steps to achieving a successful and fulfilling life at home and at work. You are the only one responsible for what happens to you. This is a story about how to stop blaming others for the way your life is now and how to take control of your own destiny.

Again, I am going to be completely honest with you. This is going to be hard work. It will not happen overnight. You will need to be consistent, focused and realistic. You will need to rise above the naysayers and the battery drainers; you will need to believe in yourself and you will need to believe in your dream.

If you're up to that challenge, I commence by asking you…what's next for you?

Chapter Two
"WHAT'S NEXT FOR YOU?"

"It's amazing what a dream can do."
FERNANDO SOTO

I taped a piece of paper to the inside of my toolbox at work. On it were four simple words: What's next for you? Every time I opened the box, I saw the sign. Every time I reached in for a hammer or a screwdriver, I read the sign. Every time I put something back in its place, I looked at those four small words- four small words that have made the biggest difference in my life.

Four small words that constantly reminded me to think ahead- to look ahead- to dream.

Those four words were a constant reminder that I am the only one responsible for what happens in my life. Like many people, I blamed others for my mediocre existence. I always thought that my mother and father were to blame for the way my life was turning out. It wasn't until I decided to choose what was next for me that I changed the way I thought. Once I decided to figure out what was next for me, I could identify and follow my dream and once I put my dream front and center, I was able to finally stop blaming others and take control of my own life.

WHAT'S NEXT FOR YOU?

So…what's next for you?

What's Next For You?

Try this. Write "What's next for you?" on some index cards and tape them to the front of your refrigerator, your bathroom mirror, on the dashboard of your car, or on the inside of your toolbox. Tape them in places where you will be sure to see them. Not only does this help you focus on and get used to putting your dream front and center, but it lets other people know that you are working on becoming the best you can be.

If you dislike what you do for a living, or are generally unhappy with your life, the people you know will know it. In fact, they already do. It shows in the work you do, the way you interact with others, and how you spend your time. Imagine, again, waking up in the morning, leaping out of bed and racing out the door to go to work. You are confident and satisfied with how you spend your days. You can't wait to see what the day has in store for you. Work is more than just work; it's a place where you are valued and respected. Going to work means stepping into a world that is challenging, stimulating and rewarding. You are a valued employee or maybe you're the boss. It's what you want to do. It's where you want to be. Imagine all of those things happening every single day.

What are you waiting for? Ask yourself: What's next for me?

When I was in high school, my dream was to become a professional basketball player. When I left high school, I had no direction. My dream of becoming an athlete dissolved away, too. I gave up my dream and my life was slowly falling apart. I wandered aimlessly, without direction and without my dream. I was lost.

"What are you waiting for? Ask yourself: What's next for me?"

So, the next thing I decided to do was pursue knowledge and education. I had to learn more. I had to go back to school and finish my high school education. I earned my GED and then I went to community college. I took general studies classes and found myself skimming the shelves at my local library and bookstores. I took a sociology course and interviewed all kinds of people, including members of my family. My political science classes introduced me to C-SPAN, The Cable-Satellite Public Affairs Network and I became a government junkie. I followed state representatives and senators. I learned about our local, state and federal governments. My business classes led me to where I am today, and even though I never graduated from college, I earned my degree in life. The classes I took spilled over into my life. A diploma was replaced with a trip into the real world to find the things I needed to get to where I wanted to be.

For me, a little bit of knowledge was motivating and exciting. All of the classes I took ignited my dream and kept my desire to achieve it burning all the time. It was a dream I hadn't yet nailed down, but the pieces were falling into place long before I knew what the whole puzzle would even look like.

Think back over your life. Take a few minutes and relive some of the tough times. If you're lucky, there haven't been too many. Focus on how you felt when things weren't going well for you, when things weren't going as planned. Visualize what happened; question why it happened. Without blaming others or yourself, simply just picture in your mind the times when you felt angry, frustrated, sad, or helpless.

Now take a break, stand up, stretch…listen to some music.

Think back over your life again, but this time, visualize a time when you were happy and successful. Maybe it was that winning touchdown in high school, the really good grade on a paper you wrote, or the day you proposed to your spouse and he or she said yes. Maybe your best day was the birth of one of your children. Whatever it was, spend time thinking about how it made you feel. How no matter what went wrong everywhere else in your life, this one shining moment was yours and it brought the rest of your life up to a higher level. Nothing could stop you.

Which exercise did you like better?

The second, correct? That's what I thought…me, too.

WHAT'S NEXT FOR YOU?

When I examined my life, I realized two things: One...I wanted to feel happy, satisfied and fulfilled all of the time and in all areas of my life. Two...I also realized that it's not what happens to us or what we do, but what we do about or with those events that makes all the difference in our lives. Having a dream gave my life the purpose it needed. Having a dream made me see that things could get better.

That's how it all started for me. I was bored and tired with what I was doing for a living. I wasn't satisfied with the way my life was turning out. I showed up every day and worked as hard as I could, but deep down inside I knew I wanted better. My dream gnawed at my brain and annoyed me while I slept. I fantasized living my dream. I saw myself happy, satisfied and fulfilled.

It was awesome!

I decided that that's where I wanted to be in the next five years. I wanted to be on the other side of the desk. My dream mattered to me. My dream was going to get me the life I wanted. The more successful I imagined myself to be, the more I wanted to be successful. The happier I saw myself, the more I wanted to be happy.

Stand in front of a mirror and take a long, close look at yourself. Not for 10 seconds; not for a minute or two...just stand there for a while and really look at yourself. It's been said that our eyes are windows into our souls. Look into your eyes and feel the joy you've had in your life. Really feel the happiness. Focus on one thing that has made you happy.

REALLY HAPPY.

Make it into a bigger than life moment and now, ask yourself...

What's next for me?

Do it. Do it now.

If you own a car, then chances are you've had this happen to you. You're out shopping. Your car is parked in a large, crowded parking lot on a busy Saturday afternoon. Everyone has places to go and things to do and so do you. Your list of things to do is long. You unlock the trunk and put your packages in. You're already thinking about your next stop. You unlock your car door and climb inside. The key goes into the ignition and...click, click, click. Nothing.

Dead.

It's not out of gasoline, because if it was, the car would still have some life. There would be lights and the radio would work. There would be power windows and a funny growling sound when you turned the key in the ignition. Today, however, you're getting nothing at all. It's your battery and it's dead... and without the battery, the car will not start. It will not take you to the next stop on your list or to your friend's house. It leaves your car in a frozen state of going nowhere. You can change the windshield wipers, get new tires and even fill the tank with gasoline, but if the battery is dead, that car is going nowhere.

Get it?

Your dream is your battery. Without your dream - without your battery -your life stays stuck in the place you are now. Everyone around you is pulling out and moving on, but you are frozen, stuck, unhappy, frustrated, jealous, upset, angry at yourself and maybe even angry at others.

If you sit there and do nothing, things will not improve. You have to pull yourself out of the car and walk to the nearest auto supply store or call someone for help. You have to pop open your hood and write down the type of battery that is sitting uselessly beside your engine, or you have to pop open your glove box and look it up in the car's manual. Either way, you have to somehow get the money and go buy a new battery.

Your dream is your battery. It becomes what charges you and propels you through each day. Your dream is your energy source. It will sustain and motivate you. Your dream will get you where you want to go. My dream did that for me and when your battery goes dead, you go get another battery.

Dreams are like that, too.

Chapter Three
WHY WORK IS SO IMPORTANT

*"If you don't go after what you want, you'll never have it.
If you don't ask, the answer is always no. If you don't step forward,
you're always in the same place."*
NORA ROBERTS (BESTSELLING AUTHOR)

Someone once hired me because they believed in me. That person believed in me because I believed in myself. I believed in myself because I had a dream that catapulted me out of bed every morning.

It's as simple as that.

Work is a very big part of our lives. We need to work to support ourselves and our families. The money we earn pays for where we live, what we eat and what we do. Making a living is important. It may just be one of the most important things we do, but it doesn't have to be just making a living. The work we choose to do should be just that- what we choose. It should be more than just something that pays the bills. It should be something that fulfils us and makes us better people. It should be something we don't mind getting out of bed in the morning to do - something that is both challenging and rewarding at the same time.

Our work should catapult us out of bed and propel us through the day.

I'm telling you this because the amount of time we spend at work is generally more than the amount of time we spend at home. You probably know this already, but it's important to really think about the amount of time you are either satisfied and challenged or bored and miserable.

How does work make you feel? Honestly.

I know a man who had a dream to become an automotive technician. He worked on cars as a young boy and was very good at it. He spent most of his time under the hood of a car. Even as a teenager, he knew this was what he wanted to do for the rest of his life. He loved everything about cars. This was his passion.

This was his dream.

This man had a rocky start to his life and many, many setbacks. He was a troubled teen and went on into adulthood dealing with many ups and downs. He was even homeless for a while. He was lost. For years, he carried his dream in his heart and no matter what happened in his life, he always found ways to work on cars. His dream of what he believed his life could be kept his head just enough above water so that he could see the sun. He could always see his dream, no matter what took place in his life, his dream was always there.

This man never stopped working on cars and eventually found a way to go to school. He worked hard and became an ASE Certified Automotive Technician. He went on to spend his life living his dream and guess what? He is now a retired ASE Certified Automotive Technician…and don't ever call him a mechanic. He will be the first one to tell you that there is a big difference between a mechanic and an ASE Certified Automotive Technician.

This man not only held onto his dream, worked hard to achieve it and lived it, but the pride he felt in himself and his accomplishment was and will always be, immeasurable. I'm sure that some of the most happiest, memorable and rewarding days of his life were spent in pursuit of his dream and now he lives knowing he accomplished what he wanted to do in life. Did it happen overnight? Of course not, but by the time he was 40 years old, in between the really good times and awfully low ones, this man kept his dream alive and he became the man he always dreamed of being. He achieved what he set out to go get.

This is exactly what I'm talking about.

Remember that little sign with the four words I taped into the inside lid of my toolbox? The words I saw every time I opened the box to get a tool? Those four words – What's next for you? – kept me on track. That automotive technician knew at a very young age that working with cars was where it was at for him. That fueled his dream for years and years. All you have to do at this point is ask yourself what's next for you and go after what the answer is. That's what fueled my dream.

My dreams have followed me around since I was in high school, but the dream that changed my life was the dream of starting my own business. After working for years and years as an employee, I had accumulated a lot of knowledge. I knew what kinds of employers I liked working for and the ones I didn't. I figured out why the good ones were good at what they did. I saw them motivate and lead with intelligence, passion and kindheartedness. I watched. I listened. I learned…and while I was learning from my supervisors, I also made sure I was a great employee.

A great employee is many things- honest…loyal…hard-working…positive. A great employee also knows how to make his or her supervisor successful by being the best employee the company can have. When I was an employee, I made it my business to make sure my employers were successful. To be a great manager and leader, you must first become a great employee.

"To be a great manager and leader, you must first become a great employee."

I looked at myself in the mirror and was pleased because I had accomplished that. I knew I was working as hard as I could. I knew I was fair, honest and loyal. I knew my work was benefiting my supervisor and the company I worked for and because of that, as I continued to look into that mirror, I also saw a strong, kind, innovative and creative leader. He was in there somewhere…and when I started focusing on my dream, I found myself focusing on the things that I needed to achieve the dream of starting and owning my own company. My dream was to take everything I learned up to this point about work, people and life and turn it into a successful business that I would be proud of.

Today, I own a contract janitorial services company. It serves professional commercial, industrial and institutional establishments. It was built on the premise that pride in the workplace includes not only the quality of the leadership and the people who work there, but also the condition of the physical environment. It's a small family-owned and operated business that's staffed with caring and professional people. I believe it's important to communicate openly with my prospective and current clients, so we do. Those open lines of communication make the working relationship more honest and personable.

What you see is what you get with me. There aren't any hidden agendas. If my clients aren't happy with something, we fix it- immediately. That's the benefit of having a good working relationship with the people I work with and for. In fact, one of our company's brochures lists these words right across the front: Leadership, pride, excellence, communication, conviction, passion, trust, respect, expertise, quality, dependability, care and satisfaction. I live and breathe every single one of these promises every single day and so must the people that work with us.

When I screen prospective employees, I ask many, many questions. I want to know more than what they could do. I want to know who they are…inside…deep down inside. I want to know what they're true objectives are, because people need to be happy with themselves. That happiness often hinges on what you choose to do in life. The success of my business depended on the quality of employees I hired.

Sam Walton, founder of Wal-Mart, built the world's largest retail business on that same premise. He started out by constructing a strong foundation of the right people. Walton believed that the success of his business hinged on the quality of his employees. [2]

WHAT'S NEXT FOR YOU?

I believe that too and that's why I spend so much time getting to know my staff before I hire them. I'm investing in much more than an employee or someone who will work hard for me. I'm investing in a person with dreams and aspirations of their own.

People who come into a business with their own dreams are ready to do their best. They're motivated. They understand how important a dream is.

Time to Say It: What is YOUR Dream?

Really...what is it? When you are not happy with your life, it will show at work. That's why identifying your dream and working hard to achieve it is so important, even if you never make it! Your happiness and success in life depends on you pursuing your dream! I've shared my dream with you. Now it's time for you to share yours. What is it, really? Have you figured out what it is yet?

You've already written down the words *"What's next for you?"* on little cards and taped them to your refrigerator and other places you will see them. You've already looked into a mirror and really given those four amazing words a lot of thought. Now it's time to think about what your dream is.

What is it? Write it here.

_____

_____

_____

When I began working toward my dream, I read hundreds of books written by successful business leaders and inspirational people. I have to say that I attribute my success, passion, drive and desire to one man: Napoleon Hill. Reading his work helped me believe in myself and when I believed in myself, I transformed my life.

Napoleon Hill (1883-1970) was an American author who believed that dreams are the cornerstone of success. He wrote and spoke about how important it is to know what your dream is and then go after it with purpose. Hill was born in a one-room cabin. His family was very poor and his mother died when he was only 10 years old. He went on to become a journalist and a successful attorney. He then became one of Andrew Carnegie's advisors. Carnegie (1835 -1919) was a very successful American entrepreneur and businessman. He inspired Hill, who then went on to spend more than two decades writing and speaking about his own philosophy of success. He was one of the first people to say that if you can think it, you can do it. [3]

Hill not only knew first-hand what it was like to start at the bottom and work his way to the top, but he studied how other people became successful, as well. He wrote many books, but the one that inspired me the most was *Think and Grow Rich*. Originally published in 1937, this book turned my life around. It was in reading Hill's words that I came to realize that everything has to start with a desire. I could have a dream, but my dream had to be fueled by a burning desire. That desire then had to translate into an overpowering obsession. Hill's book inspired me to become the man I am today. I recommend you read it and while Napoleon Hill's work changed my life, many other people and success stories helped me, too.

I learned about how important a positive attitude is from John Maxwell, who is a bestselling author and expert on leadership. I learned about goal setting from reading books by Tony Robbins, a motivational speaker and life coach. My point is, we can all learn from others. Go to the library and read. Go online and find cool blogs.

Learn. Be inspired.

I heard a recording of Napoleon Hill once. He was lecturing about success and told a story about Thomas Edison. He said that Mr. Edison told him once that if he hadn't succeeded at inventing his "incandescent electric lamp" he'd be back in his laboratory working on it instead of wasting his time talking to Hill.

Besides Thomas Edison, Hill interviewed more than 500 successful people about their secrets of success, including Alexander Graham Bell and William Wrigley.

WHAT'S NEXT FOR YOU?

Read something inspirational today. You will be amazed at how much it will help you fuel your dream.

Education goes beyond what we learn in school. For me, my true education began when I started looking at and learning from the people around me. Books helped a lot and if you have access to a computer and the Internet, the resources are limitless, but you don't have to have a computer or Internet at home, your local public library has these resources for you to use. Use them. That's what they're there for.

Here's another car metaphor.

The global positioning system, GPS, in my car is always one step ahead of me. On its little screen, I can see where I am, how fast I'm going, the time I will arrive at my destination and what my next turn will be. I know that in about 3.5 miles I will be making a left turn onto I-95. That's a comforting feeling, especially when I am unsure of where I am or driving in an area I am unfamiliar with. Reading about how other people succeeded and the mistakes they made along the way is like a global positioning system. It alerts us of what to look out for and what lies ahead. Reading other people's success stories also targets the things they did right. Good examples. Great inspiration. One of the great things about learning how others reached their dreams is that you realize that you're not alone. You realize that there are many others with a pursuit of their own.

Everyone has dreams.

The big difference is that not everyone has the drive, inspiration, motivation and burning desire to make their dreams a reality. It's a lot easier to do nothing and if you're still reading this book, then I know that you're one of those people with the desire and drive to succeed. As Napoleon Hill said, "let no one stand in your way."

Remember that automotive technician? I am 100% certain that some of the most happiest and rewarding days of his life were spent in pursuit of his dream and now he lives knowing he accomplished what he wanted to do in life. You can do that, too. Just ask yourself what's next and identify your dream.

Lets go back to the note in my toolbox.

I own a successful business and when I turn my computer on every morning, these four words are still staring at me: What's next for you? It worked once and continues to remind me that I am not only living my dream, but have the opportunity and drive to seek out another one if I want to. Reading those four words takes me back, but it also propels me forward. It helps me remember and reminds me to keep moving.

It has given me a winning attitude and as John Maxwell would say, "attitude isn't everything, but it sure is the difference maker."[4]

Chapter Four
ATTITUDE MAKES A DIFFERENCE

"The greatest discovery of all time is that a person can change his future by merely changing his attitude."
OPRAH WINFREY

Oprah Winfrey. You'd have to be living without a television your entire life to not know who she is. Oprah is an American talk show host, actress and publishing icon. She has been called the greatest black philanthropist in history. Her compassion, vision and wealth have influenced millions of people's lives. Oprah Winfrey's unsinkable, unstoppable, selfless and enthusiastic attitude made her who she is today.

Born in 1954 in Kosciusko, Michigan, Oprah's mother was an unmarried teenage girl. Her early years were hard, but she lived on a farm with a loving grandmother who nurtured and supported her. When she turned six years old, however, her life changed. Sent to live with her mother in Milwaukee, Oprah was sexually abused for four years by male relatives and another man. The abuse started when she was only nine years old. She ran away from home and eventually became pregnant and gave birth to a son, who died a week later. She then went to live with her father, Vernon Winfrey, in Nashville, Tennessee.

Oprah's father was strict, but saw her potential for greatness. He made her go to school and stick to a curfew. In addition to her studies, he asked her to read and report on one book a week. Vernon helped his daughter pick up the pieces of her life. He saw qualities in Oprah that no one had seen or nurtured since she was living with her grandmother as a young child, and it was through his encouragement and direction that Oprah was able to turn her life around. Vernon believed in her, but it was Oprah herself and her strength of character and attitude that carried her even further. Like her father, Oprah knew at a young age that she had always been destined for greatness and that's what attitude is all about. [5]

Attitude is huge. It's bigger than a great work ethic. It's stronger than the desire to do well. Attitude is what takes you to the top. Winston Churchill had it right. He once said that attitude makes a big difference. It does and Churchill is in good company. Leaders in all walks of life agree that attitude is everything.

Thomas Jefferson was a big believer in the power of a positive attitude. He once said, "Nothing can stop the man with the right mental attitude from achieving his goal." [6] Ted Turner, American businessman, media mogul and founder of CNN, the cable news network, said that he'd never run into a guy who could win at the top level in anything today and didn't have the right attitude. Turner goes on to say that becoming a success also depends on giving it your all, being prepared and thinking things through, but attitude is also a big part of it.[7] Napoleon Hill takes it a step further when he said, "Your mental attitude attracts to you everything that makes you what you are."[8]

Would you continue seeing a doctor or dentist if he or she had a poor attitude? How far would that negative attitude go with you when it comes to your health and well-being or the health and well-being of your family? Would you let a mechanic with a poor attitude work on your car? Would you date or marry someone with a poor attitude? Would you hire someone with a poor attitude? Merriam-Webster's online dictionary defines attitude in a few different ways. It says attitude is a "mental position, feeling, or emotion toward a fact or state; a negative or hostile state of mind; or a cool, cocky, defiant, or arrogant manner." Roget's Thesaurus offers words like demeanor, mindset, philosophy, point of view, reaction, character and temperament as synonyms for attitude. While those definitions and words are accurate, I have my own definition of attitude.

Attitude is having a positive and open mindset. It is being able to rise above the small stuff to get the big stuff done. Attitude is knowing that you have what it takes. Someone with a great attitude is someone who is respected and respects other people, listens and responds in a mature way and puts aside personal issues for the good of everyone.

A great attitude opens doors. It really is one of the keys to success.

"A great attitude opens doors."

I'd like to share with you a sad but true story about what can happen when a poor attitude prevails, but let me further explain what a poor attitude is.

A person with a poor attitude has the ability to work hard, but doesn't like to be told what to do. He or she creates strife, has all the answers and tends to burn bridges. Even though he, or she, may be a productive individual and may produce good numbers for the employer he works for and takes pride in the work he does, no one really wants to work with him, because a negative attitude - more often than not - causes coworkers to overlook all the good. Positive character traits and valuable contributions are cancelled out by a poor attitude.

A poor attitude causes doors to close.

I once hired someone I know personally to work at my company. I hired him at entry level. I gave him every opportunity to explore and figure out the best way for him to contribute to the company. He and I talked about management opportunities and even a partnership, but not one of the positive employment outcomes were ever realized by him because of his poor attitude. From day one, he questioned and second guessed everything I did and the way I ran my business, and while I am open to suggestions, this man's approach was so negative he never made eye contact with me. At times, he'd even walk away in the middle of a conversation. While the quality of his work was top notch and extremely superior, it took him more than twice as long to complete a task than his coworkers. I attribute this to his terrible attitude. His negativity caused him to complain and waste time. He only saw the faults in others and this has cost him many personal and professional relationships. His poor attitude overshadowed the fact that he was a great and hard-working employee. People, like this man, who let their attitudes ruin their work and life are not going anywhere. They are stuck and as a result, their quality of life suffers, too.

But there's hope.

Work on seeing things in a positive way. Stop blaming other people for the way your life has turned out. Take a good look at yourself and make adjustments if you need to, and above all, work on maintaining a positive attitude.

As an employer, I am always willing to give someone with a great attitude a chance...

...and I do.

A great attitude is important for getting ahead, maintaining relationships and achieving your dreams, but a great attitude is also necessary in order to keep yourself above the naysayers.

There will always be people out there who may not want to see you succeed. Adversity is inevitable, but failure isn't. People will always doubt you no matter where you are in life. A strong, positive attitude will help you navigate around the pressure and the critics. Some call this having a thick skin, I call it attitude.

A positive attitude matters.

So get one and get moving.

Chapter Five
NEVER SETTLE

"Once you say you're going to settle for second, that's what happens to you in life."

JOHN F. KENNEDY

Baseball.

There's nothing more exciting than sitting in the stands and watching your favorite team fight its way to the top. Every game – win or lose – is a short story in itself to be retold the next day at work or around the dinner table. Sometimes that story is told again and again for months. We watch baseball on television and listen to it on the radio. We are drawn to it. We love it. The athletes standing on the field and taking their turns at bat are our heroes. They bring us joy and sorrow and they inspire us. Our athletes even sell us cars, cereal and sneakers. Our athletic heroes motivate us, because the game is that important and we stop everything else and pay attention. We find the time to fit our passion for baseball in, no matter what, but it doesn't have to be baseball.

It can be football, hockey, tennis, golf, or skiing. The sport you prefer is whatever your passion dictates. The athletes who play are the ones who inspire you.

Right now, I bet you can list at least three athletes who inspire you and if you're not a sports fan, then think of three musicians, or performers, or writers, or entrepreneurs. Go ahead. I'll wait. Do it right now. Who inspires you?

1. _____

2. _____

3. _____

Now…look at the names you wrote down. Can you think of one thing they all have in common? One thing that sets them apart – in your mind - from the thousands of others who do the exact same thing they do?

Is it their passion? Drive? Motivation?

From my own experience, it's probably a combination of all three. It's no accident that people like Mickey Mantle, Tiger Woods, or Eli Manning are so good at what they do. Most professional athletes – or ballerinas, rocket scientists, journalists, rock stars, politicians, presidents, CEOs and actors – discover what they want to do in life, fall in love, become hooked and put everything they have into being the best that they could be in their chosen field.

They ate, slept, breathed and lived their dreams.

New York Yankee Mickey Mantle, considered by many to be the greatest baseball player who ever lived, once said, "During my 18 years I came to bat almost 10,000 times. I struck out about 1,700 times and walked maybe 1,800 times. You figure a ballplayer will average about 500 at bats a season. That means I played seven years without ever hitting the ball." [9]

Cool way to look at motivation and passion, because with those odds, Mantle's motivation and passion for baseball kept him at the top of his game for 18 years. He kept showing up at the ball field, ready to play and while athletes are great examples of motivation because of their public profiles and celebrity status, it's interesting to note that, in Gallup's poll of the most admired people in America in 2011, the list of the top 10 men and women do not include even one athlete.

Top 10 Most Admired Men and Women in 2011[10]

MEN	WOMEN
Barack Obama	Hillary Clinton
George W. Bush	Oprah Winfrey
Bill Clinton	Michelle Obama
Rev. Billy Graham	Sarah Palin
Warren Buffet	Condoleezza Rice
Newt Gingrich	Laura Bush
Donald Trump	Margaret Thatcher
Pope Benedict XVI	Ellen DeGeneres
Bill Gates	Queen Elizabeth
Thomas Monson	Michele Bachman

What's even more interesting is the list of people most widely admired by Americans in the 20th century. Topping the list of this poll, also conducted by Gallup, is Mother Teresa, Martin Luther King, Jr., John F. Kennedy, Albert Einstein and Helen Keller. Almost half of all Americans chose Mother Teresa as the one person they admired most. In this mix of men and women from different walks of life, it is really cool to note that the one thing they all have in common is that they devoted their lives to helping other people, as opposed to acquiring great wealth or power. There is nothing wrong with the acquisition of wealth and power, if that is your dream. It just wasn't theirs. The things that motivated people like Martin Luther King, Jr. and Albert Einstein are not the same things that motivated Babe Ruth or Sally Ride and they are not the things that motivate you or me. We are all motivated by different things and those different things are our dreams.

Motivation is natural when you're in pursuit of your true dream. Many people have contributed to society in pursuit of their dreams and as a result, we consume their products and/or ideas each and every day. Many of the ideas we take in can be used to help us pursue our own dreams, too. Once your desire to achieve your dream consumes everything you do and see, read and hear, your dream becomes an obsession and you'll always be motivated. Once you begin chasing the one thing you really want to do in life, motivation will naturally follow.

"Motivation is natural when you're in pursuit of your true dream."

Think about the first time you fell in love, for instance. Remember that all-consuming and wonderful way you felt when the two of you were together and how that person continued to consume your thoughts when you were apart? You were excited thinking about him or her. You would do almost anything to make him or her happy. The world seemed brighter and you were invincible. Being with the person you fell in love with took zero motivation. No one had to talk you into spending time together. No one had to twist your arm to call him or her. The feeling of falling and being in love was enough and if you had to make a list of all the things you had to do and put them in order of importance, being with the person you love would be at the top of the list.

Motivation will do that.

Remember Napoleon Hill from Chapter Three? Remember I said that he wrote *Think and Grow Rich*, the one book that has inspired me the most to live my dream? Well, Napoleon Hill and his book, *Think and Grow Rich,* inspired me the most because in it he says that it really is the thoughts that count. If you think you can do something, you can. It's that simple. His whole system of success is based on drive, desire and a laser-focused eye on the dream. Of course, there's a little bit more to it than that, but after reading his book, success is attainable for anyone who knows exactly what they want, believes they can do it, and are willing to do the work to get there. [11]

You just have to believe and you can't let anything stop you.

Ever.

WHAT'S NEXT FOR YOU?

On New Year's Eve in 2009, snowboarding Olympic hopeful, Kevin Pearce, slammed his head during a practice run in Park City, Utah. The 22-year-old from Vermont had just missed a new move and cracked his helmet on the icy course. He was rushed to a hospital and placed in a medically-induced coma because his brain injuries were so severe. For two years, the young snowboarder slowly healed. Unable to walk, talk and remember the accident, Kevin faced a lifetime of physical therapy, impaired vision and memory loss. Snowboarding was something he once did and would never do again.

Until December 13, 2011.

In front of a crowd of friends and fans, Kevin Pearce got back on his snowboard and took three trips down "Springmeier," a tame trail sandwiched between the "Swinger" and the "Powerline" at the Breckenridge Ski Resort in Colorado, and he did it with style. According to an Associated Press story that ran the next day, Kevin kicked up "just enough powder behind him to remind people that, yes, this kid can still ride." [12]

Kevin Pearce still has a long road ahead and he is aware of that, but he also knows that what kept him going during the challenges of learning to walk and talk and ultimately learn to snowboard again was the dream of being out on the mountain again doing what he loves most. It was that intense motivation that drove him to work as hard as he could and stay focused and so, 712 days of pain, tears, sweat and support from his family and friends paid off. Kevin is one of the thousands of stories out there proving that motivation and hard work is everything.

These are the stories you should be spending your time reading.

Vince Lombardi, one of the greatest and most inspirational football coaches of all time, once said, "Winning is not everything - but making the effort to win is." [13] Whether you watch ESPN or CNN, admire the guys and gals who hit the balls, the ones who make the laws, or the ones who give shoes to children in countries where they have none, there is one question you need to ask yourself.

How motivated am I?

Close your eyes and imagine yourself living your dream. Take a few deep breaths and enjoy the feeling. Think about how life would look to you and how living your dream makes you feel. How motivated are you to live that life?

On this scale, mark where you are now. Be honest.

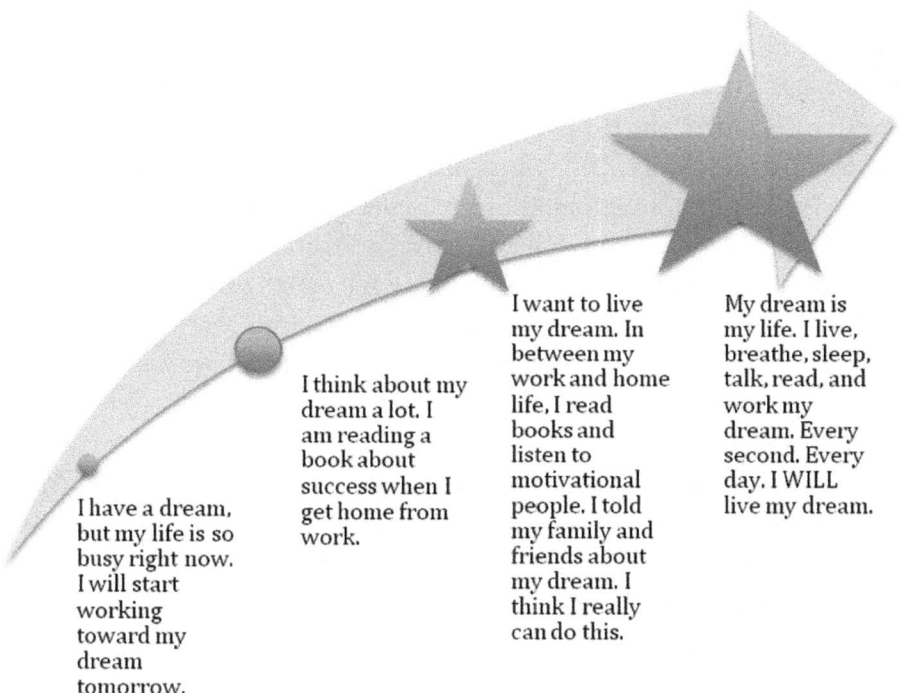

I have a dream, but my life is so busy right now. I will start working toward my dream tomorrow.

I think about my dream a lot. I am reading a book about success when I get home from work.

I want to live my dream. In between my work and home life, I read books and listen to motivational people. I told my family and friends about my dream. I think I really can do this.

My dream is my life. I live, breathe, sleep, talk, read, and work my dream. Every second. Every day. I WILL live my dream.

You don't need me to tell you that if you marked anywhere on this shooting dream star except where the biggest star is, you are falling a little short in the motivation department. This is not to make you feel bad about yourself. This is to make sure you understand that going after your dream is a decision that cannot be taken lightly. It is not for the faint of heart. It is a decision and commitment that must be fueled constantly by desire, obsession and drive.

It is a decision that must be fueled by motivation.

In 1943, a psychologist, teacher and author named Abraham Maslow (1908-1970) wrote a paper. It's a famous paper that outlines his theory of motivation and a theory that is still used today by business leaders. Maslow's Hierarchy of Needs looks like a pyramid. At the base of the pyramid is the most basic of needs. These are physical needs like food, water, sleep and air. According to Maslow, these are the things that absolutely need attention. A person is extremely motivated to meet any one and all of these needs because they are the ones we need to stay alive. Once our physical needs are met we need a safe place to live, a job, a savings account and the ability to pay for health care. Moving up the pyramid, Maslow describes social needs like having positive friendships, falling in love and being a part of a group and other needs like recognition, accomplishment, self-respect and attention. At the top of the pyramid are the things we all strive for: truth, justice, the meaning of life and wisdom. This top triangle is what really makes people happy. Maslow said that people are motivated by their unsatisfied needs. He says that as long as we are always moving toward becoming more satisfied, we are healthy and have the potential to be happy. [14]

I have shared Maslow's Hierarchy of Needs with my daughter, but instead of using Maslow's needs, I tell her about a different hierarchy of needs. I ask her to picture in her mind a pyramid filled with personal values. On the top of the pyramid are the things that are the most important to us. On the bottom of the pyramid are the things we care nothing about. The things that we value the most are the things that require zero outside motivation. Here's an example. Let's pretend a high school senior is being pressured by her parents to go to college. She goes because she knows it's what her parents want her to do, not because it's something she sees as valuable and important. Education is high on her parents' values pyramid and low on hers. Because this student does not value education like her parents do, it will require a good amount of motivation for her to do well. The interest level in excelling will probably not be there.

My own daughter takes great pride in both her studies and her personal appearance. She wakes up two hours before school and spends a lot of time getting ready. No one has to tell her to do this. She just does it. She also spends time at night doing her homework and studying. Her mother and I do not have to prompt or remind her to get her schoolwork done. Like personal hygiene, getting good grades is high up on her values pyramid. Both of those things require zero motivation for her to do, but doing her chores is an entirely different story. They require an enormous amount of motivation for her to get those done. This is the same for you and your dreams. If you really want something, you will find a way to make it happen.

The one really great thing about motivation is that you can have it with you wherever you go. You can carry your dream in your mind while you're working, cooking, fixing your car, babysitting, or doing any of the hundreds of other things life has us doing, but remember this one thing: It is absolutely crucial for you to constantly feed your dream and motivation is one of the most important things your dream needs to grow into reality.

One of the many jobs I once held was operating equipment in a factory. I was in pursuit of my dream, so every spare minute I would get, I would spend reading motivational books. Once I'd set up the machine to run, I would head over to my book and read a few paragraphs. Then I would go check on the machine. I would do this over and over again, all day long. Reading even just those few paragraphs was motivating to me. This motivation made me happy and I would perform better at work. This constant nourishment of motivation made me work harder and faster. It made me a better employee while turning me into the person I wanted to be at the same time.

Fuel Your Dream

You have your dream. You are excited and focused and ready to do everything you can to get to where you want to be. Here are seven things you can do to stay motivated while you are doing un-motivating things:
1. Listen to an audio book or motivational speaker while you are driving in your car.
2. Put on headphones and listen to a great speech or a how-to book while you are working (as long as you're permitted to do so).
3. Have a conversation with a good friend about your dream.
4. Write down your dream and post it where you can see it.
5. Picture yourself living your dream.
6. Watch movies that motivate you.
7. Listen to music that gets you excited and motivated.

WHAT'S NEXT FOR YOU?

Your own success is in your own best interest, no one else's and if you don't follow your dream, no one else is going to make sure that you do. You have to stay focused. You have to find ways to push forward. You have to keep going. You have to stay motivated.

You just have to.

Chapter Six
INSPIRATION AND INFLUENCES

"People are always blaming their circumstances for what they are. I don't believe in circumstances. The people who get on in this world are the people who get up and look for the circumstances they want, and, if they can't find them, make them."
GEORGE BERNARD SHAW (1856-1950), PLAYWRIGHT
AND FOUNDER OF THE LONDON SCHOOL OF ECONOMICS

Inspiration.

It comes from many different places. Sometimes it's a quote, sometimes it's reading a chapter in one of Napoleon Hill's books about success, and sometimes it comes from the people you spend time with.

I once heard someone say, "Tell me who you spend the most time around and I'll tell you what you'll become in the next 10 years." I think Napoleon Hill even said it in some form in his book, *Think and Grow Rich*. It means that if you are not focused enough on what you want in life, you subconsciously become what you hang around the most. When you are seriously pursuing your dream, your influences should be inspiring.

WHAT'S NEXT FOR YOU?

I looked the word *inspiration* up in a dozen dictionaries and found that the word *influence* was always somewhere in the definitions. I believe that's because inspiration and influence are inseparable. The only thing to remember is that influential people are not always inspiring, but inspiring people almost always influence us.

There's a great book out there called *Start Something That Matters.* It's written by a young entrepreneur named Blake Mycoskie who started his own company in 2006. Blake's company, TOMS Shoes, donates a pair of new shoes to a child in need for every pair he sells. Inspiration for this business venture happened while he was on a trip to Argentina earlier that year. There he met children without shoes and while that may not seem like an obvious health risk, in countries where conditions are less than sanitary, not having shoes to protect the feet makes the body extremely susceptible to illness and disease. Blake came home and put together a prototype of a shoe that he started selling to family and friends. His idea was to make a pair of shoes, sell a pair of shoes and then give a pair of shoes to a child who doesn't have one. His goal was to create a company that would give back. He was 27 years old. [15]

Blake Mycoskie says he wrote his book, *Start Something That Matters,* in 2011, to inspire other people to find what matters to them and go out and start something that makes a difference, too. Blake says his inspiration comes from many places, including a favorite quote by Ghandi: "Be the change you want to see in the world."[16]

Wow. Isn't that amazing?

Blake Mycoskie's book is not the only inspirational reading material out. There are tons. For me, more than 90 percent of positive influences came from books. When I knew exactly that my dream was to be self-employed, there was not one person close enough to me who had done that. Even within my own family, there was no one who understood how I felt because they had never dreamed of doing the same thing and while family members were supportive and meant well, their influence could've very easily caused me to stray from my goal. There are many distractions in this world and you will need an enormous amount of concentration and dedication to fulfill your dream.

Sometimes that can be the most challenging when dealing with the people who love you the most…or people like Harry.

> **"There are many distractions in this world and you will need an enormous amount of concentration and dedication to fulfill your dream."**

Years ago, when I worked at a manufacturing facility and was in pursuit of my dream, a coworker, whom I will call Harry, came up to me in the cafeteria during lunch and said loudly, "Hey Fernando, where you gonna build your business… Fantasy Land?" I carried on and continued to pursue my dream despite Harry's negative comments. He was one of many people that shed nothing but a negative perspective on my aspirations. Well, I recently bumped into Harry at work. Only this time, he was doing the same thing he did for work more than 10 years ago and my company was at his facility performing our services. His employer is one of our clients. Now, being at a job for a long time is not a bad thing if you are happy, but Harry was very unhappy and dissatisfied with his life. I ran into him in the cafeteria one night and he asked me how I "ended up doing this?"

I said, "Harry, I own the company."

Harry's face got red and he mumbled an "oh." In the few minutes we talked, he didn't have one positive thing to say about the company he worked for; the company that gave him paid vacation days, sick days, personal days, bonuses, holiday parties, company outings and a great, brand new facility to work in. He was still complaining about the same things he grumbled about 10 years earlier. He was where he was in life because he did nothing to change it. He would rather moan and groan than find a way out.

Be careful.

People like Harry are all around you. Not everyone has a positive outlook and very few people will care about you and your dream. In fact, in one company where I worked that had almost 300 employees, only four people made me feel good about my aspirations and the effort I put in while working toward my dream. Two were managers and two were co-workers.

One of the biggest lessons I learned throughout all of this is that even family can stand in the way of your success. I know this sounds awful because who loves you more than your family and friends? These are the people who want what they think is best for you. The only problem is that what works for them may not always work for you. Plus, there's the whole dream thing. Your dream and what you want to achieve in life is tailored to you and you alone. Family and close friends mean well, but for all kinds of reasons they tend to sometimes stand in the way of what you want to do. It's fine to share your dream and confide in family, but not a good idea to go to your family for 100 percent of the support you are going to need. They love you, but they may not have the experience to advise you or the inspiration you need.

That's why I turned to books.

Fernando's Top Ten List of Inspiration and Influence Authors
1. Napoleon Hill
2. Robert Kiyosaki
3. George Clason
4. J. Paul Getty
5. Tony Robbins
6. Sam Walton
7. Richard Branson
8. Russell Conwell
9. John Maxwell
10. Zig Ziglar

For suggestions about what to read by these inspirational authors, please see "Cool Stuff to Read" at the end of this book in Appendix A.

Reading books written by smart, inspirational and successful leaders is an excellent way to get motivated. Another great way is to find like-minded people to talk to and places to go to learn and hear more. I would strongly advise mingling and associating with people who have your same interests. Study them first. Get to know them. If they are positive, then share some of your ideas with them over time. See what they have to say. People who listen carefully and believe in you will be the ones who will make you feel important and inspired. Use this principle on people you come in contact with every day. Really check out the people you know at work, school, home and out in the world. Only associate yourself with people who are positive. Be careful about sharing your dream with negative people. In fact, don't do it. We all need inspiration from time to time, but in the marathon of racing toward your dream, inspiration is everything.

> *"The toughest part of getting to the top of the ladder,*
> *is getting through the crowd at the bottom."*
> UNKNOWN

Who is the crowd at the bottom of your ladder? Better yet, who is at the top? Who are the people you can look to for encouragement, advice and inspiration? If you can name at least one person right now, you are doing great and as you work toward your goal, your list of inspirational influences will grow and grow.

1. _____

Finding the right influences – the right circumstances - will inspire you to do what it takes to get to the top of your ladder. Be the person who keeps looking for the right inspiration. Never give up. Finding inspiration will help you answer that one question we've asked again and again: What's next for you?

Chapter Seven
ARE YOU READY TO LIVE YOUR DREAM?

"The real secret of success is enthusiasm."
                                                    WALTER CHRYSLER

Think enthusiasm. Think pink.
   Mary Kay Ash, female entrepreneur and founder of the cosmetic company named after herself, learned how to be successful at a young age. After being turned down for promotions at the company she worked at for 25 years so many times she lost count, Mary Kay looked back on her childhood and on four important words she learned from her mother, "You can do it." Armed with those words and a positive attitude, she built a successful cosmetic company from the ground up. Literally.
   Defined as an extreme devotion, an absorbing control of the mind by anything you find interesting and are in pursuit of, enthusiasm is another kind of fuel for your dream. Mary Kay's dream was fueled by it.

From an early age she was encouraged by her mother to believe that she could do anything she set her mind to. That kind of encouragement means more than gifts, money and possessions. It is the mortar that binds the bricks that builds the foundation that we then build our lives on and if you are lucky enough in your life to have had that kind of influence at a young age, then you have the ability to believe in yourself. [17]

We already talked about how Oprah Winfrey's life was changed by her father's influence. Mickey Mantle, one of baseball's greats, was most influenced by his father, too. Former President John F. Kennedy was also influenced by his father, Joseph Patrick Kennedy. Early influences in your life go a long way in building confidence and self-image. These influences go a long way in building a life you dream of. In fact, studies show that positive influences make a difference.

For example, in a 2004 Duke University study, researchers found that what parents do and say really matters. The children whose parents were more involved in their schools, helped them make decisions regarding classes and talked with them regularly about their friends, classes and lives had higher aspirations than children without that kind of influence. The cool thing was that it didn't matter what the parents did for a living. It all boiled down to involvement, support and encouragement. This study and many others recognize the key role loving, caring parents play in our lives. [18]

We know that when children are very young, parents and family are the greatest influencers. As children move into adolescence, they must draw on the lessons they learned at home and build on them to interpret the influences of their classmates and peers. Friends at school become more important influences than parents. This generally carries through into young adulthood and by the time we are in our twenties, many of us have a foundation of beliefs and feelings about ourselves that we draw on when we interact with other people and make decisions about our lives. Mary Kay used her strong sense of self and confidence in her ability to be and do whatever she wanted to in life to build her company. After being passed over again for a promotion by her employer, she went home and sat down at her kitchen table. She made two lists. One was a list of all the policies and actions she believed worked well for companies. The other list was things she thought needed improvement. Mary Kay studied both lists and realized she had just taken her first step toward creating her own business. She had written her very first business plan and with the help of her 20-year-old son, an initial investment of $5,000 and her can-do attitude, Mary Kay created her beauty product and consultant company for women. That was in 1963 and she ran her company the way she ran her life. Mary Kay committed her leadership to the women she employed by encouraging them. Her business philosophy was based on the idea that all women can be successful and achieve their potential in whatever they want to do.

Mary Kay used the words her mother instilled in her – *you can do it* – every day. She was an inspiration to everyone around her and to all the people she employed. She believed in the courage and acquisition of dreams and when she died in 2001, she left behind a company that still lives on and carries her view of the world. Mary Kay herself once said: "The real success of our company is measured to me in the lives that have been touched and given hope." Do you see what she did right there? She reached down inside and drew from the reserves of encouragement she had stored; the hope and attitude she had acquired as a young child. She used the words her mother said to her to build an empire that encourages women to be stronger, productive and more successful.[19]

Influences and Other Factors

Think of one person who you believe has been a positive influence in your life. It has to be someone you know; someone in your life from the past or present. Write that person's name here:

_____

Good. Now spend a few minutes thinking about how that person influenced you. I know, I know, you had to write this same kind of essay in the fourth grade, but here's the thing – there's a reason why teachers get kids to think about these things. They are important. The people we admire and who influence us make us better people. So, in keeping with the spirit of this chapter, please write five words that describe the person you named above:

1. _____ ;   2. _____

3. _____ ;   4. _____

5. _____

Look at the five words you just wrote. How many of those words would you use to describe yourself? How did the characteristics and influences of the person you named above affect your life?

Courage. Hope. Inspiration. Self-confidence. A strong foundation. All of these things are important factors in achieving your dream. But Mary Kay's extraordinary success story was fueled by one more major factor: Enthusiasm. Look around you and think about the enthusiastic people in your life. Enthusiastic people have energy and passion. They ask questions and listen to the answers. They are curious, positive and LOVE what they do. People with enthusiasm are emotionally connected and joyful. They laugh often. They find what they love to do and they do it. They have a desire to serve a purpose and live for others. They place value on honesty and sharing. Enthusiastic people are good influences.

"Enthusiastic people are good influences."

There are two basic kinds of snowstorms. There is the kind where the flakes are huge and swirl around crazily as they fall from the sky. Storms like these are cool to watch. They are busy and exciting and make you think they will never end. Now think about the other kind of snowstorm. This is the kind where the flakes are small and float steadily to the ground. There's not a lot of activity out there, just a slow, steady barrage of small snowflakes. No busy swirling and twirling. No drama.

WHAT'S NEXT FOR YOU?

So how does this relate to enthusiasm? Well, some people wear their enthusiasm on their sleeves. They are intense and focused and get the job done in a way that may be kind of like the big swirling and dramatic snowstorm. Then there are the people who are just as enthusiastic. They are intense and focused and get the job done in a way that is more like the smaller, steady snowflakes. The end result of both storms is snow cover on the ground. The result is just reached in different ways.

In his book, *The Law of Success in Sixteen Lessons,* Napoleon Hill wrote: "Enthusiasm will so energize your entire body that you can get along with less than half the usual amount of sleep and at the same time it will enable you to perform from two to three times as much work as you usually perform in a given period, without fatigue."[20]

That's enthusiasm! It's that never-give-up, never-die attitude. It's the I-will-stop-at-nothing-to-get-what-I want behavior. Whatever catchy hyphenated version of enthusiasm you can come up with, it all boils down to one thing: Having the right attitude and the intense focus and energy you need to reach your goals and achieve your dream.

Are you ready?

Are you ready to start living the life you want? Are you ready to begin seriously and enthusiastically chasing your dream? Let's find out. Look over the list of words below and check all that apply to you right now.

- ☐ Excited
- ☐ Motivated
- ☐ Inspired
- ☐ Great attitude
- ☐ I'm ready
- ☐ Serious about success
- ☐ Focused
- ☐ Obsessed
- ☐ Relentless
- ☐ Brave

> ↪ If you checked ALL the boxes, you are ready to begin the journey. Get some fuel, hang on and get ready for the ride of your life.
> ↪ If you checked 6 to 9 of the boxes, maybe you should reread this book and actually fill in the writing prompts instead of just answering them in your head.

✍ If you checked 5 or under boxes, I recommend you first think seriously about your dream. Ask yourself "What's next for me?" and then meditate. Think long and hard about what it is you want out of life.

I end this first section of my book with two more words about enthusiasm: Howard Schultz. Yes, he is the man behind the Starbucks coffee empire, but did you know that Starbucks was Starbucks before Schultz got involved? It was a small, trendy coffee shop in Seattle, WA. Back in 1981, while working for Hammarplast, a Swedish company that made and sold kitchen equipment, Schultz noticed that one of their clients was buying up drip coffeemakers like they were going out of style. This peaked Schultz's curiosity and he paid the small coffee company a visit. In his book, *Pour Your Heart Into It*, Schultz describes his first visit to Starbucks. Reading about Schultz's first experience with Starbucks coffee and the enthusiasm it generated catapulted him and the company into worldwide success. [21] At the end of 2011, the company's website noted that there were 16,858 Starbucks stores up and running, with the newest located in Hungary and El Salvador. [22]

See what a little enthusiasm can do?

Now it's your turn. The next section of this book will teach you everything you need to know to chase and achieve your dream. I have to warn you again, though, that this adventure is exciting, mind-blowing, exhausting and will test you in many ways. Hang onto your dream because your obsession and motivation, strong will and desire will lead you to places and cause you to do and think of things you've never done and thought of before. Soon you will be living the life you are dreaming of now.

Wow.

Are you ready?

Here we go...

PART TWO

Chapter Eight
THE PERSONAL TIMESHEET

"By changing nothing, nothing changes."
Tony Robbins

Get ready.

You have your dream. You know exactly what you want. You can picture it in your mind. You can see yourself living the life you want. You are reading some books. You are talking to people.

Now what?

You've gotten this far. You're still reading. I can help. But first, let's go back and review.

WHAT'S NEXT FOR YOU?

Dreams are the fuel that propel growth. Without an aim in life, there's nothing really pushing you to be the best you can be. We can philosophize all we want about the meaning of life and why we are all here, but the bottom line is this: the world out there - the world we see in front of us - was built by people like you and me. Everything out there that has been made by man or woman was once a thought in someone's mind. Skyscrapers. Toys. Cars. Cell phones. Shoes. You name it and someone saw it in his or her mind's eye and made it a reality. Our passions have created the world we live in and guess what? Everyone is allowed to participate and contribute. We all hold a ticket to what's out there. We all have the potential to play in the same playground.

You have to believe that.

This chapter is all about the ready. Getting ready to chase your dream, catch it and succeed. There are a number of things you will need to do. The first part of this book was the pre-game show. It provided some background. It pumped you up and hopefully got you ready, but now it's your turn. It's time for you to get in the game.

It's time for you to contribute.

It's time for you to be happy; to live the life you want; to have your dream come true.

When I was ready to have my dream come true, I knew I had to dive in with both feet. I was committed, motivated, enthusiastic, focused and obsessed. I knew I had to do something different if I wanted to move forward. I knew I had to organize my time and my life.

I needed to change some stuff.

I needed to make time to read and learn all I could. I was already closely observing my supervisors and taking everything in. As I've said before, a dedicated and focused attitude goes a long way. All employers and business owners want their business to succeed. They all want to do a good job and often times, the way that manifests itself is in the way the people they work with and supervise do their jobs. Being a good employee is good for everyone. Being an employee who listens and learns and goes the extra steps is good for you. I was already doing that when I decided to go after my dream. I just needed to fit the pursuit of my dream into my work schedule and life. I needed to roll up my sleeves and now it's your turn to roll up yours.

The very first thing you need to do is take a personal assessment of what you do with your time. In other words, it's time to analyze the way you spend your time.

Time management is an art. It is learning how to organize your time, your day and your life so that you are efficient and productive. Learning to manage your time is like filling a warehouse with everything you need to build your dream. Time management takes discipline, organization, planning, goal-setting, prioritizing, scheduling, monitoring how you are doing and analyzing how you spend your time right now. People spend thousands of dollars to hire people to help them manage their time. You don't have to do that…you have me. I'm going to help you figure out what you have to do and how you can find the time you will need to pursue your dream.

Time management is one of the keys to success. There are thousands of books dedicated to getting your life organized and your time under your own control. Procrastination is an art form for many people and having the world at our fingertips any time we want, day or night, is both a blessing and a curse. How distracting are the millions of games, videos, news stories and social sites on the Internet? You really have to limit your time to doing the things you must do to reach your dream. Between the things we have to do, the things we want to do and the things we like doing, our days are overflowing. We find ourselves making choices all the time, choices that can keep us where we are or help us to move forward; choices that at this stage of your journey are critical to your success.

Think about a typical day. In fact, think about today. List the things you have to do today. Maybe it's taking a shower and going to work. Maybe you have to go to an interview for a new job or you have a doctor's appointment. Whatever it is that you must do today, write it here:

WHAT'S NEXT FOR YOU?

NEEDS

_____

_____

_____

Now write down all of the things you like to do that you typically find time to do during the day. Do you like surfing the Internet? Write it down. Do you enjoy infomercials, horror movies, or reality television shows? Write it down, but only write it if you actually find yourself doing these things at least once a day. These are not wants, they are likes.

LIKES

_____

_____

_____

Okay, good. Now write down the things you wish could find time to do: your wants. This box can include wanting to read a book you've been putting off, writing that novel you have in your head, or learning to speak another language. Whatever it is, write it here. Please note that wants are not the same as likes. A like is something you actually find time to do during the day. A want is more about something you wish you had the time to do.

FERNANDO L. SOTO

WANTS

_____

_____

_____

This exercise hopefully got you thinking about time management. Time management is a choice. It is not something you typically learn how to do in school. It's one of those things that you learn out in the world. Maybe it should be taught in schools, though. Time management is that important.

Ambrose Bierce (1842 – 1914), an American journalist, once wrote: "Day, n. A period of twenty-four hours, mostly misspent." Isn't that the truth? Just stop and think about all of the things you do in the course of a day. You get up and maybe you take a shower. You eat breakfast. Maybe you make your lunch. You go to work. You work all day, come home and eat dinner. Maybe you shower at night instead of in the morning. You watch television, help your kids with their homework; you go out with friends. You pay bills. You do your laundry. Whatever it is that you do, you are probably wasting a little time somewhere, every single day.

Don't get upset…we all do it. How we spend our time says a lot about who we are. The hour you may waste during the day could be spent studying, reading, or networking your way into your new life. You need to find out how you spend your time in order to find and put those lost minutes to work. That's why I created a personal timesheet, to track what you do during the day and for the next two weeks, you will use the timesheet to track your time.

WHAT'S NEXT FOR YOU?

Take a few minutes to study the Personal Timesheet on the next page. As you can see, there are 48 half-hour blocks. This is where you get to write down everything you do in a 24-hour period of time. Do you sleep four, eight, or fourteen hours a day? Naps are included as sleep. Do you spend 16 hours a day at home, watching television, cleaning the house, playing with your kids, or playing on your computer? Do you spend time doing nothing at all?

Fill in the time sheet. You can do this as you go through your day or at the end of the day. I recommend carrying it with you and updating it four to six times a day or two to three times, whichever works for you. It is important to complete the form as accurately as you can. Be sincere. This form will help you create the time you will need to realize your dream. Please don't skip this step. After charting how you spend your time for 14 days in a row, you will have in your hands a valuable new tool. This valuable tool – completely filled in 14 times!

"Dost thou love life? Then do not squander time, for that is the stuff life is made of." – Benjamin Franklin

"Do not wait; the time will never be "just right." Start where you stand, and work with whatever tolls you may have at your command, and better tools will be found as you go along." – Napoleon Hill

FERNANDO L. SOTO

Personal Timesheet

Name:		Date:
Personal Timesheet		
12:00 AM		
12:30 AM		
1:00 AM		
1:30 AM		
2:00 AM		
2:30 AM		
3:00 AM		
3:30 AM		
4:00 AM		
4:30 AM		
5:00 AM		
5:30 AM		
6:00 AM		
6:30 AM		
7:00 AM		
7:30 AM		
8:00 AM		
8:30 AM		
9:00 AM		
9:30 AM		
10:00 AM		
10:30 AM		
11:00 AM		
11:30 AM		
12:00 PM		
12:30 PM		
1:00 PM		
1:30 PM		
2:00 PM		
2:30 PM		
3:00 PM		
3:30 PM		
4:00 PM		
4:30 PM		
5:00 PM	8:30 PM	
5:30 PM	9:00 PM	
6:00 PM	9:30 PM	
6:30 PM	10:00 PM	
7:00 PM	10:30 PM	
7:30 PM	11:00 PM	
8:00 PM	11:30 PM	

SUMMARY BOX

Category	Hours

WHAT'S NEXT FOR YOU?

Fourteen days. That's right. You heard me. For the next two weeks, I want you to take time to accurately and honestly fill out your personal timesheet. It will reveal exactly how you spend your days. It will uncover places where you will be able to borrow time, eliminate certain activities, or multi-task. If you want to change your life, this is where it begins. That's because time is the one thing the day doesn't have enough of. If you waste your time, abuse it, or don't have enough of it, you will need to be extremely resourceful with it.

Don't waste another minute that you could be using to chase your dream. Start logging those minutes right now.

While you are working on finding the time to follow your dream, just remember: Your dream is what will propel your growth. Don't be afraid. The world is waiting to hear about your passion. The cycle of life out there continues. Laws are passed every day. Government officials come in and out of office. People enroll in and attend school. Businesses are started. New things are invented. People are entertained. You and your dream are next. Isn't it time?

"With the right choices and changes, you will realize your dream and be living the life you envision for yourself."

Napoleon Hill once compared life to a checkerboard. He said that your opponent on the other side of the board is time. My personal timesheet will help you outwit time to win the game. With the right choices and changes, you will realize your dream and be living the life you envision for yourself.

Just keep asking yourself: What's next for me?

Chapter Nine
CHANGE IS GOOD

"Motivation is what gets you started. Habit is what keeps you going."
JIM ROHN (AMERICAN SPEAKER, AUTHOR)

While you are busy filling out your personal timesheets for the next 14 days, there are a few more things you can do to get ready. It's time to "get set" and that means putting yourself in a position of positive power. Reread the chapter on motivation and attitude if you don't remember how important it is to be positive and focused on your dream. You will be changing some of the ways you do things now, and it may take some time to adjust to spending your time in different ways, but change is good.

Change. It's exciting and challenging and scary and really good for us. It means breaking a habit or two. It means mixing up the way we are used to doing things. Change is almost always hard, but that's only because things that are worth doing usually take hard work and effort. It's supposed to be hard. Think of it this way…if it was so easy to live your dream, everyone would be doing it and everyone isn't. That just really means that the people who are focused and motivated and willing to do everything it takes are the ones who make it. I can attest to that. I can also say that all the hours of focusing and reading and working and never losing sight of my dream paid off. I am living proof, but as Tony Robbins said, "By changing nothing, nothing changes."

"Change is almost always hard, but that's only because things that are worth doing usually take hard work and effort."

Tony Robbins is best known for his self-help books and dynamic theories about how to live the life you want. He is sometimes criticized for his methods, but continues to influence many, many people on their journeys to being the best they can be. Robbins believes that if people continue to do what they have always done, the results will continue to be the same. In pursuit of my own dream, that piece of advice has appeared so many times, worded in so many different ways by so many different motivational speakers and business leaders that I feel like I can reword it, too. My version of the "nothing will change unless you change something" advice goes a little like this.

Once I knew that my dream was to own my own business, I became obsessed. That obsession with reading and learning and doing everything I could to achieve my dream life brought out a change that I hadn't expected. I became laser-light focused on getting to where I wanted to be. My life revolved around my dream. Everything I looked at and talked about related to my dream. I became dedicated to my dream. That dedication turned into a way of living, a way of trying to express what I wanted.

Dedication. It's very similar to sticking to something and seeing it through, but it involves more than just effort. It requires 100% of all you've got. I learned the meaning of the word dedication when I went after the life I am leading now. I learned that dedication means operating at full throttle. It means saturating yourself in the material so much so that you are even dreaming about it at night when you go to sleep. I believe with all of my heart and soul that if you don't try, you can't win.

Jim Rohn (1930-2009) was an entrepreneur, author and motivational speaker. He is one of the many rags-to-riches success stories floating around in the be-all-you-can-be world. Born on a farm in Idaho with a strong work ethic, Rohn went with a friend to hear a motivational speaker as a young man. He was 25 years old and the speaker was Earl Shoaff. [23]

Now, Earl Shoaff (1916-1965) was a successful entrepreneur himself. He was president and chairman of the board of the Nutri-Bio Corporation, which was a company that sold vitamins, minerals and dietary supplements through direct sales. He was also the founder of Ovation Cosmetics. Shoaff has been credited with influencing many business leaders and motivational speakers, including Jack Canfield, Brian Tracy, Mary Kay Ash and Zig Ziglar. When Shoaff and Rohn met, Shoaff challenged him to reach a goal. Within six years, Rohn did. Rohn then moved to Beverly Hills, California and told his story in a speech to a rotary club there. That speech, entitled "Idaho Farm Boy Makes It to Beverly Hills," was a huge success and led to more speaking engagements. Eventually, Rohn changed millions of lives with his inspirational and motivational books, programs and presentations. [24]

In one of his Rohn's books, *Five Major Pieces to the Life Puzzle,*[25] which was published in 1991, Rohn says that how we think, how we feel and what we do are three of the four key ingredients to living the kind of life we want. The fourth ingredient is self-monitoring, or constantly evaluating where you are and how you are doing. In chapter 11, I will explain and show you how to use my Daily Worksheet. In a nutshell, it is a way to keep track of what you need to do. It will help you prioritize and keep track of your time, as well as help you prepare and plan for your day. I use this daily worksheet every single day and frequently have three or four going at the same time. I know we are all not the same, but I really believe you will come to find this a useful tool and I can't wait to share it with you. Again, like Tony Robbins said, "By changing nothing, nothing changes."

It's no surprise that success is all about doing things in a certain way. Sometimes people get lucky and strike it rich fast, but that really doesn't happen all that often. In fact, that sort of thing rarely happens. Most of the people at the top of their game got there by working hard, focusing on what mattered most and brought them results and by sticking to their convictions. It's no surprise that success is hard work and no matter how you say it, success boils down to changing something in order to make room for something else to happen.

Change: Same sentiment, different words.

I've said it before and I will say it again and again. Obsess about your dream. Surround yourself with positive influences. Submerse yourself in the wise words of successful leaders. There are books, eBooks, books on tape, famous quotes and blogs. All are great ways to stay pumped. Here are 10 great quotes about change, success, sticking to it and never giving up.

1. "If you do what you've always done, you'll get what you've always gotten." (Tony Robbins)

2. "Twenty years from now you will be more disappointed by the things that you didn't do than by the ones you did do. So throw off the bowlines. Sail away from the safe harbor. Catch the trade winds in your sails. Explore. Dream. Discover. (Mark Twain, 1835-1910; American author)

3. "It's not whether you get knocked down, it's whether you get up." (Vince Lombardi, 1913-1970; American football coach)

4. "The difference between a successful person and others is not a lack of strength, not a lack of knowledge, but rather a lack of will." (Vince Lombardi, again)

5. "Action and reaction, ebb and flow, trial and error, change - this is the rhythm of living. Out of our over-confidence, fear; out of our fear, clearer vision, fresh hope. And out of hope, progress." (Bruce Barton, 1886-1967; American politician, advertising executive, author)

6. "Change before you have to." (Jack Welch, b. 1935; Chairman and CEO of General Electric from 1981-2001, author)

7. "Never believe that a few caring people can't change the world. For, indeed, that's all who ever have." (Margaret Mead, 1901-1978; American anthropologist)

8. "Your life does not get better by chance, it gets better by change." (Jim Rohn)

9. The winners in life think constantly in terms of I can, I will, and I am. Losers, on the other hand, concentrate their waking thoughts on what they should have or would have done, or what they can't do. (Denis Waitley, b. 1933; American motivational speaker, author)

10. "The problems of the world cannot possibly be solved by skeptics or cynics whose horizons are limited by the obvious realities. We need men who can dream of things that never were." (President John F. Kennedy, 1917-1963)

I look at chasing your dream this way: as you race toward what you want, even if you trip and fall, you are still moving forward and because Napoleon Hill and his books played such a huge role in my success and the way I look at life and dreams, I will add one more great quote. Hill once said, "Man, alone, has the power to transform his thoughts into physical reality; man, alone, can dream and make his dreams come true."

Are you making your dreams come true? Are you honestly and earnestly completing your time sheets? I hope you are. Those 14 worksheets will shed much light on what you will need to do to succeed.

Your success will not be an accident. It will not be like winning the lottery. Your success will be hard-earned and much appreciated. In the next chapter, I will help you analyze the results of your timesheets and help you plan and manage your time. In the meantime, let's go back to the all-important question: "What's next for you," because always going back to those four words is what staying focused is all about. The success of all of the work you will do boils down to those four words. Those four words are the foundation for the home where your dream lives and grows and from those four words come my five basic and simple steps to success.

Step ONE: Have a Dream

You are still reading, so you are still chasing the dream you have. The dream that defines what you want out of life. This is the first step because it is really the most basic. If you don't have a dream, other people will define who you are. If that happens, you could end up being a product of something else…

something you may not want to be or do. I believe you should be the product of what you have specifically and thoughtfully chosen to be. You should be what you set out in life to be.

We all should. Our happiness depends on it.

I know someone who worked for 33 long and hard years for the same employer. This type of thing isn't as common any more as it used to be years ago, but it does happen. He landed this job in his youth. It was with a fairly decent-sized company and he decided to stay there for more than three decades of his life. He was just let go of not too long ago and now he is in a situation where he has to start all over again. He gave it all to this company and now he is out in the world of unemployment. If you asked him today if that job was what he wanted to do his whole life he would probably say no. Maybe that job was not what he aspired to do and yet he stayed there and ignored any aspirations that may have arisen in the years he was devoting to that company. Think about how quickly time passes us by and how we would feel in a similar situation?

When you look back, you should feel great pride in what you have done with your life. You should be happy with who you are and the things you've accomplished. Just remember that employers will never put the dreams of each of their individual workers ahead of their own company's mission. Good employers care and they show it in many ways, but companies in general are not in existence to help employees achieve their dreams. It's your job to do that. Your career or job may be important to you, but is it really what you want to do? You know, if it's not, you're hurting the company just as much as you're hurting yourself. You have to ask yourself that question many times. Am I doing what I want to do? You have to be honest with yourself. You have to listen to your answer and while I am not suggesting that you quit your job, I am telling you from the bottom of my heart that you will be the most happiest when you are in pursuit of your dream. You should be where you are now because that's where you have specifically chosen to be.

So have that dream and use the tools in this book and go for it.

Step TWO: Focus All Attention on Your Dream

I know I've said this many, many times so far, but that's how important step two is. You have to focus on your dream in order to achieve it. You must devote the majority of your spare time and energy to the pursuit of your dream. Keep in mind that nothing worthwhile happens overnight. This is going to take motivation, dedication and the obsessive desire to succeed. This is not for the weak of heart. If you don't play, you will not win. If you don't invest in yourself, you have a zero percent chance of seeing any kind of a return and if you are not interested in devoting your time to reaching and living your dream life, then you are not chasing the right thing.

Chasing a real and true dream is like falling in love. You can't wait to leap out of bed and race toward it. The time you put in feels effortless because you are certain it will lead you to the life you want to live. Even though you spend many hours thinking about and working on your dream, you don't mind because you love the way it feels to work toward happiness.

In 2010, a man named Mike Wolfe took a passion he had for history and turned it into his dream business. A lover of antiques as a child, Wolfe spent most of his life in barns, abandoned houses and junkyards looking for treasures that other people discarded. Wolfe even sold a prized antique motorcycle to finance his own bicycle shop in Eldridge, Iowa, but what Mike really wanted to do in life was capture the people he met and the diverse experiences he accumulated on the road. He successfully found a way to do that and was granted his own television program on the History Channel, *American Pickers*. He asked his childhood buddy, Frank Fritz, who was working at the time as a fire inspector, to join the show and it generated so much interest and enthusiasm that it landed Mike on the cover of *Entrepreneur* magazine and maybe you don't see yourself on the cover of any business magazine, but you should if that's what you want. [26]

Christine Comaford-Lynch, author of *Rules for Renegades*, is an entrepreneur and writer. She was the first woman programmer for Microsoft and as of 2012 built and owned five businesses and was advisor to 36 start-up companies. In her book, she tells about a picture that she hung over her desk before she started her first company. It was a picture of one million dollars. Christine's dream was to make a lot of money and she focused on that picture and on her dream every minute of every day. She looked for networking opportunities and made life-changing decisions based on her quest for the life she wanted to live. She was devoted to her dream and that's just what you have to be, too, devoted, by focusing all of your attention on your dream.[27]

Step THREE: Stay Away From Naysayers

One of the most important things you need to do while you are getting ready to pursue your dream is to surround yourself with positive influences. Naysayers are everywhere and just having positive people around isn't enough. You will need to avoid the negative comments and influence of these naysayers. Steer completely clear of them. They will bring you down. That's a guarantee and what they will do is take your dream, pick it apart and splay out everything that could go wrong. Naysayers only see the negatives. They will never give you the encouragement and support you will need on your journey. They work against you, not with you.

Remember how I said that we all become what we are around? Some people mean well. Some people don't. It's your job to figure out who you can let in. This is the quest of your life and ultimately the quality of your life depends on it. The concentration and dedication you will need to proceed means that you must eliminate the distractions and negative people are the first to go. Always remember that you are your own boss when it comes to the things that will affect you. You are the only one in charge of your success. So stop thinking negatively and accept the fact that other people are under no obligation to support and encourage you. You are going against the grain here. You will definitely encounter naysayers.

J.R.R. Tolkien, in his book *The Lord of the Rings*, wrote a scene between two characters, Frodo and Bilbo. In it, Bilbo warns Frodo about venturing forward. He says, "It's dangerous business, Frodo, going out your door. You step onto the road, and if you don't keep your feet, there's no knowing where you might be swept off to." [28]

Keep your feet. Don't let the battery drainers shut you down.

Step FOUR: Stick With It!

That's really all I need to say here. Stick with your dream. Give it time. Don't give up.

It's been said that successful people make decisions promptly, stick to their decisions, wait to see the results and then move on. On the other side of the coin, unsuccessful people tend to be indecisive, slow to make decisions and change their minds often. Unsuccessful people are scared and afraid to commit. Don't you do that. Don't get paralysis of analysis. Give your decision the thought it deserves and needs, consider the facts, weigh the options, make your decision and move on.

Go.

From my own experiences, the busier my company started to get, the faster I had to make decisions. I knew that my clients did not want to wait around for a week to hear my response. In a fast-paced environment, quick turnaround and promptness is important. That's how I built my business- prompt rectifications to any concerns; prompt responses to any questions, but I also knew that in order for my office to run, my employees needed my attention, too. There were days when question after question came my way and I couldn't sit nervously in a corner contemplating, debating and waiting for an answer to come to my head. I had to step in, make decisions and provide answers. I had to lead.

This leads me to another important part of pursuing your dream. You will need to be brave. You will need to be in charge, in control and learn as much as you can as you go along. You will need to stand straighter and act smarter because people will begin to look up to you. They will admire what you are doing. Enjoy that. Take pride in it. Your supportive and positive friends, coworkers and family members will be interested in what you are doing and what's happening to you. In your network, you will find yourself somewhat of a mini celebrity. As you go through your days, you will pick up momentum. You will be so proud of yourself someday.

WHAT'S NEXT FOR YOU?

Step FIVE: A Great Attitude

I believe a great attitude is the icing on the cake. It is the one thing that will pull all the other steps together. When life gets in your way or battery drainers intervene, your positive attitude will carry you over the finish line. Your consistency and motivation, coupled with your great attitude, will make you the success you dream of becoming.

The Five Simple Steps to Success
1. Have a dream
2. Focus all of your attention on your dream
3. Stay away from naysayers and battery drainers.
4. Stick with it
5. Have a great attitude

Now let's see how your timesheets look. It's time to get going.

Chapter Ten
STAYING ON TRACK

"You will never 'find' time for anything. If you want time, you must take it."

CHARLES BRUXTON (1823-1871;
ENGLISH PHILANTHROPIST, WRITER)

Times up. Before you, in your hands or spread out on your kitchen table, are 14 pieces of information that will help you realize your dreams. Analyzing how you spend your time today is a big part of changing how you will spend your time tomorrow and how you spend your time tomorrow is a big part of making the commitment to throw yourself into chasing and ultimately living your dream.

So, let's take a look at those timesheets. Was it hard to fill them out? How did it feel to keep track of your every waking moment? For me, filling out two weeks of timesheets was a real eye-opener. Time has a way of slipping by and before you know it, you have spent more hours doing a whole lot of nothing and all those hours add up. So when I asked you to record the things you normally do every day, it was for you to see exactly how you spend your time.

WHAT'S NEXT FOR YOU?

Being honest with yourself is so important, especially at this great and exciting turning point in your life; especially now as you chase your dream. That's because you will need to rely on your own integrity and resources. You will need to rely on YOU.

It's kind of like joining Weight Watchers.

Ranked as one of the most successful weight loss programs around, Weight Watchers has been around for more than 40 years. Started in Kean Nidetch's living room in Queens, NY, millions of people use the program and its meetings and products to lose weight today. [29] There are many reasons why this weight loss program is successful, but one cornerstone of the program is the daily tracker. Members are encouraged to write down or record online everything they eat throughout the day. They calculate their points and see how they are doing. If their points go over their daily allotment, they generally do not see a weight loss. If their trackers show that the amount of foods they are eating are healthy and within the recommended point range, members are likely to see a weight loss.

That's kind of like the personal timesheet you just filled out.

Weight Watcher members are also encouraged to attend weekly meetings. These meetings are led by members who have successfully reached their goals. They know what it feels like to want to lose weight and have learned how to do it safely and smartly. So, think of me as your leader. I have been where you are now. I learned how to successfully get to where I wanted to be and I am here helping you do the same. Millions of Weight Watcher members can't be wrong.

Let's analyze your timesheet.

Here's what a typical workday might look like. Notice I am just focusing right now on what you do from midnight until you leave work.

12:00 AM Sleep
12:30 AM Sleep
1:00 AM Sleep
1:30 AM Sleep
2:00 AM Sleep

2:30 AM Sleep
3:00 AM Sleep
3:30 AM Sleep
4:00 AM Sleep
4:30 AM Sleep
5:00 AM Sleep
5:30 AM Wake up, shower
6:00 AM Eat breakfast, watch News
6:30 AM Check email, Facebook, Twitter
7:00 AM Drive to work
7:30 AM Arrive at work, have coffee with Tim and Jon
8:00 AM Work
8:30 AM Work
9:00 AM Work
9:30 AM Break – 10 minutes (coffee with Mark)
10:00 AM Work
10:30 AM Work
11:00 AM Work
11:30 AM Lunch…go out for sandwich
12:00 PM Eat and read newspaper
12:30 PM Back to work
1:00 PM Work
1:30 PM Work
2:00 PM Work
2:30 PM Break – 10 minutes (snack from vending machine)
3:00 PM Work
3:30 PM Work
4:00 PM Work
4:30 PM Work
5:00 PM Drive home

Before we go any further, here's a word about sleep. Sleep is important. Studies show that most adults need between seven and eight hours of sleep

WHAT'S NEXT FOR YOU?

each night on a regular basis to function well, but we all have experienced times when we are not getting enough sleep at night because we are sick, worried or are awakened by things around you like noises, cats, or children, among other things. Not getting enough sleep drains you and builds up over time. So, for example, you may get four good, solid nights of sleep, but still feel tired because you had a week where your sleep was interrupted or less than six hours a night. Lack of sleep can get in the way of your productivity, memory, performance and mood. When you don't sleep well, you are not as alert.

So why am I telling you this? Look at your timesheet. You are the only one who can decide if you are getting enough sleep or if you can wake up an hour earlier each morning to read and work on your dream. This is the one area where I am not qualified to tell you what you can do. Just know that sleep is a very important and vital part of being an alert and productive person. If you have to scrimp on time, then maybe sleep is not the place to do it.

In looking at this one sample timesheet, I can already find at least two hours that can be used toward chasing your dream. Now let's look at the other half of this same timesheet.

5:00 PM Drive home
5:30 PM Eat dinner
6:00 PM Mow grass
6:30 PM Help kids with hw
7:00 PM Help kids with hw
7:30 PM Computer time
8:00 PM Computer
8:30 PM Watch football on TV
9:00 PM Watch TV
9:30 PM Watch TV
10:00 PM Sleep
10:30 PM Sleep
11:00 PM Sleep
11:30 PM Sleep

Please remember that this is just ONE day. In order to really figure out where you can eliminate certain activities and add ones that help you do the things you need to do to live your dream, we need to look at all fourteen timesheets. But before we do that, I want to show you how to use the Summary Box. The Summary Box on each timesheet is where you get to tally up your hours. The activities you categorize in this box must always add up to 24 hours. For example, here's what the summary box might look like:

SUMMARY BOX

CategoryHours

Sleeping7 1/2

Work9 1/2

Driving3

Housework2

Kids2

Here's the thing about the Summary Box. This is going to be as individual as your day. This one looks like this. Yours will most definitely look like something else. Sum up the activities that cost you the most time, like sleep, work, driving, babysitting, etc. Write down what the activity is and then just add up the hours for each day. Once you have done that fourteen times, list the activities that take up most of your time and tally them all up. Your sheet may look something like this:

Sleep	112 hours
Work	126 hours
Driving	42 hours
Kids	28 hours
TV/Computer	28 hours
TOTAL	336 hours

There are 336 hours in 14 days. If you take the number of hours for each activity and then divide it by the 336 hours, you will get a percentage that tells you how much time you invest in each particular activity. So, using the

WHAT'S NEXT FOR YOU?

numbers above, if I divide 112 hours of sleep by the 336 hours within a 14-day span, it tells me that I sleep 33% of the time.

112 ÷ 336 = 0.33333

The decimal 0.33333 has to be turned into a percent. To do that, you move the decimal point two spaces to the right and then replace it with a % sign. Drop the zero. So, 0.33333 becomes 33.333. You can round that out to 33% and that means you sleep, on average, 33 percent of the time, or about 1/3. Let's try another example.

If you added up your work hours and got 126 hours and we divided that by 336, this is what you would get:

126 ÷ 336 = 0.375

126 ÷ 336 = 037.5

126 ÷ 336 = 38% ⟹ This means that work took up 38% of your time.

What this formula does is give you a macro glimpse of how you regularly spend your time. Of course, week to week, the numbers may change slightly, but this is a good, overall and fairly accurate snapshot of how you use your time. Using the list above, here are the calculations for the rest of the activities:

Sleep	112 hours	33%
Work	126 hours	38%
Driving	42 hours	13%
Kids	28 hours	8%
TV/Computer	28 hours	8%
TOTAL	336 hours	100%

Okay, now let's take the same number of hours for each activity and divide them by 14. This will give you the average hours per day you spend on that particular thing. For example, let's go back and look at sleep. Your total time spent sleeping over 14 days is 112 hours. If we divide 112 hours by 14, we get 8 hours.

112 ÷ 14 = 8 hours

That means you spend an average of 8 hours each day sleeping. Moving on through each activity again and dividing them by 14 days, here's the breakdown of how many hours you spend doing each thing...on average:

Sleep	112 hours	8 hours each day
Work	126 hours	9 hours each day
Driving	42 hours	3 hours each day
Kids	28 hours	2 hours each day
TV/Computer	28 hours	2 hours each day
TOTAL	336 hours	24 hours in a day

What does this all mean? For starters, remember that your chart and your percentages will not look like mine. Time is extremely valuable. We each need to budget our time carefully, but because you are getting ready to chase your dream, budgeting your time is now an extreme sport. By using the formulas above and studying the data, you now have a fairly good idea as to what kinds of activities are consuming most of your time. Is it sleep? Work? Time spent surfing the Internet and watching television? From here on forward, you will need to train yourself to follow a strict time budget. Life is short and your dream is big. The reality is that from this moment on, things will have to change. The way you spend your time will have to change and depending on what your timesheets reveal, they may need to change a lot.

How to Make a Change

Making a change in the way you are used to doing things can be difficult. Here are a few ideas and tips that may help get you going:

* ★ **Write down your goal**. State it clearly and connect it to your dream. For example, I might write: To watch television less, play on my computer less and wake up 30 minutes earlier to make 90 minutes of time every day to pursue my dream of starting my own business.
* ★ **Make a list of the reasons why you are making a change**. Putting your reasons in writing is like making a contract with yourself. You

are confirming that your dream is important enough to make these life changes to your time and daily routines. Writing the reasons will help you realize the significance making these changes will have on your life and eventually living your dream.

* **Map out your new routine.** Just by taking that blank timesheet and filling in how you plan to spend your time will help keep you on the straight and narrow.
* **Talk to yourself constantly.** Here's where it is vital that you become your own cheerleader. Keep telling yourself how awesome life is going to be. How incredible you are and what a brave and great life change you are making. This is where you have to be mentally strong and incorporate the Napoleon Hill mentality- "the mind attracts what it dwells upon," Napoleon Hill. You have to live it until you are it, or be it until you become it.
* **Find someone else to cheer you on.** It's always good to have someone on the sidelines yelling and screaming words of encouragement. It can be your spouse, best friend, parent, or neighbor. Whomever it is... just tell them exactly what you are doing and why. Ask them for their encouragement.
* **Be prepared for the naysayers.** We've talked a little about this and will talk more about it later, but the best thing to do when someone is trying to sabotage your efforts is to tell them exactly what they are doing wrong and how it makes you feel and ask them if they could please correct it. If that doesn't work, avoid that person's company. You need to really surround yourself with positive influences.

Armed with these tips, you are ready to make that change. Grab a fresh Personal Timesheet and go on and mold your day into exactly what you need it to be. You can do it!

Study the numbers and percentages and really look closely at how you use your time right now. Plan out your days by molding timesheets to factor in your dream. You need to find one hour each day, at least, to work on your dream. You will need to shift patterns or change certain things you do.

You might even have to eliminate or cut down on other activities. It's all up to you where you can borrow time from. Using the numbers in the examples above, the first place I would trim time from is in the TV/computer category. Two hours every day spent watching television or surfing the Internet could be spent on the pursuit of your dream. Even by just cutting that time in half, you have already found one hour. I did it. So can you.

I was so motivated and excited while pursuing my dream that I made time throughout my day to work on it and there are many things you can do. You would be surprised at how much you can read in 30 minutes while eating lunch. Find a motivational audiotape or CD to pop in while driving to work. Even if you listen only half the time, you are that much further ahead. I also focused my mind on my dream. I was in pursuit of it every waking hour. I ate, drank, walked, worked and drove thinking about my dream. It consumed my life, but then again, it should.

Success is not easy. It takes hard work and dedication, discipline, motivation and time. Without the luxury of a time management coach, I had to figure it all out myself and I did. I found a way to make it work for me. You can too and remember that success is in the basics. It is the small, tiny steps you take daily that will get you there. These baby steps will get you closer to your dream much faster than huge leaps taken sporadically. Kind of like the children's folktale about the Tortoise and the Hare.

One afternoon, an arrogant and self-involved hare challenged a tortoise to a race. The hare being one of the fastest animals in the forest knew he would win and had no worries. On the day of the race, the hare decided to really show off to the other animals. He sped away from the starting line, leaving the turtle moving slowly and steadily along the forest path. Within seconds, the hare was out of sight. So, he decided to take a little nap. He figured it would take the turtle forever to get to where he was resting. It took a while, but the turtle caught up to the hare and slowly and steadily continued on. Taking small and slow steps at a consistent pace brought the turtle closer and closer to the finish line. He wanted to beat the arrogant rabbit more than anything in the world and he did. Through determination and consistency, all of the tortoise's small and steady steps paid off and the hare was humiliated.

WHAT'S NEXT FOR YOU?

The moral of the story is slow and steady wins the race. It applied to the tortoise as he wound his way along the forest paths to pass the rabbit and win the race. It applies to you right now. One hour a day will get you closer to your dream faster than a handful of hours invested one time each week. Find where you can steal time and take it. Prioritize and use your minutes wisely. Even fifteen minutes goes a long way. Don't waste your valuable time. Invest it in the pursuit of your dream.

> **"Don't waste your valuable time. Invest it in the pursuit of your dream."**

Someone once asked me what I would do if I couldn't find even one hour in my day to devote to pursuing my dream. I asked that person to think about being in love. What would you do to see your significant other? Would you give up watching television at night to spend time with him or her? Would you give up other activities during each day in order to be with that person? Of course you would. You would somehow find the time to spend with that one special person. Well, think of your dream as that one person. Find the time not because you have to, but because you want to and if you don't feel like you can, then maybe you need to re-evaluate your dream. Maybe you need to re-think what it is that you want to do with your life. Is this really the dream you want for yourself? Go back to asking yourself what's next and be really honest, because pursuing a dream is not for lightweights. It's not for the faint of heart and it certainly is not for people only half in.

It's all or nothing.

Staying on Track

Motivation is key. You are making significant changes in your lifestyle and how you are used to spending your time. Try some of these ideas when you are feeling like you are running out of steam:

- ★ Go back and reread your goal statement and the list of reasons why you are doing this. In fact, make a few copies of your dream statement and time goals and post them in places where you are apt to see them. Seeing the reasons behind your actions in print will help keep you going.
- ★ Visualize, or create mental pictures, of you living your dream life. There is actually documented proof floating around out there that says if you picture yourself in the position you want to be in and then work toward it, you will achieve your dream. It's easy enough to do and doesn't cost anything.
- ★ Recite positive affirmations once or twice a day. Positive affirmations are statements like "I am listening to motivational speeches and books every day for an hour and know I can do the things these successful people are saying." Many entrepreneurs and business leaders swear by daily affirmations.
- ★ Reward yourself. Patting yourself on the back goes a long way to keeping things going. One thing to remember, though, taking an hour off is not considered a reward.
- ★ Take things one day at a time. I know this is one huge cliché, but it's true. When we are pursuing our dream, we are excited and motivated, but we are also human. Be kind to yourself and do the best you can.

Above all, don't worry. I will elaborate on the many things you can do to keep your success moving forward in chapter 12. So stay tuned.

You need to focus and always be on the lookout for the next motivational book to read, the next person you can share your dream with and that next moment when you can tell yourself that you can do this, because...
You CAN do this!
Find the time and then tell yourself you will use it to chase your dream and your new life. Stick to your schedule and never allow anything to get in the way. The quote at the beginning of this chapter is meant to be sort of a battle cry: If you want the time to pursue your dream, you must take it.

WHAT'S NEXT FOR YOU?

Go.
Fight.
Win.

This is your life we are talking about here. Do what you tell yourself you are going to do. Stay focused and motivated and you'll get there.

You will.

Chapter Eleven
THE DAILY WORKSHEET

"Promise me you'll always remember: You're braver than you believe, and stronger than you seem, and smarter than you think."

A.A. MILNE (1882-1956)

A.A. Milne had it right. Well, actually, Milne wrote the words, but it was Christopher Robin who said them to one of Milne's best-loved characters, Winnie the Pooh. Words of encouragement that are just as good now as they were years ago.

You really are braver than you believe you are.

You really are stronger than you seem...

...and you definitely are smarter than you think.

Hey, you're still reading this book and you haven't given up on your dream. You know what you want and you now have some of the time management tools you need to get things going. You know how you spend your time and exactly when you can actually do the work to achieve your dream. So now I want to show you my daily worksheet.

The Daily Worksheet is just a simple tool to help you keep track of and remember the important dream-related things you need to do. Now that you

WHAT'S NEXT FOR YOU?

have created time using the personal timesheet, you should begin to rely on the Daily Worksheet to keep you on track. This is the worksheet dedicated to the pursuit of your dream and reserved exclusively for your dream-related activities. That's because these are the activities that absolutely, positively must get done. No excuses. Remember the slow and steady tortoise? Your daily worksheet is your tool to get across the finish line. Take a look at it on the next page.

"A dream doesn't become reality through magic; it takes sweat, determination and hard work." – Colin Powell

"In order to succeed, your desire for success should be greater than your fear of failure." – Bill Cosby

FERNANDO L. SOTO

Daily Worksheet

Date:

High Priority (20%/80% Results)	Business Tasks
1	1
2	2
3	3
4	4
5	5
6	6
7	7
8	8
9	9
10	10
Personal Tasks	11
1	12
2	13
3	14
4	15

Appointments

5:30 AM	2:00 PM
6:00 AM	2:30 PM
6:30 AM	3:00 PM
7:00 AM	3:30 PM
7:30 AM	4:00 PM
8:00 AM	4:30 PM
8:30 AM	5:00 PM
9:00 AM	5:30 PM
9:30 AM	6:00 PM
10:00 AM	6:30 PM
10:30 AM	7:00 PM
11:00 AM	7:30 PM
11:30 AM	8:00 PM
12:00 PM	8:30 PM
12:30 PM	9:00 PM
1:00 PM	9:30 PM
1:30 PM	10:00 PM

Messaging & Notes

WHAT'S NEXT FOR YOU?

My Daily Worksheet has been modified over the years to fit my lifestyle. As you can see, there is very little space for personal tasks like mowing the lawn, going to the movies, and meeting friends for lunch, and much more room to keep track of business tasks.

I work a lot.

The point of the worksheet is to structure your day so that you do not lose focus of what needs to be done. I find that if I start my day knowing what needs to get done, I have a better chance of slowly moving forward in the right direction and that direction is always toward my dream. I know people who are constantly reminding themselves to do things, things that really should have been completed months ago. These people sometimes forget to do the most important things they need to do during the day and before they know it, it's time to go home. I never let that happen to me. I keep four of these daily worksheets running all the time. I don't do this because I want to, but because I don't want to forget the things that I know I eventually need to do. The worksheets help me remember.

For me, it works and I really think it will work for you, too.

Don't want to forget to send a card to your brother for his birthday next month? Write it down somewhere on the list. At the beginning of the day, when you check your worksheet, there will be a note reminding you about it and at the end of the day, when you check your worksheet again, you will see a note about it and again, it will remind you. If you don't get to it right then and there, then it will be on your worksheet tomorrow, when you will again be reminded. The most important thing to remember to do is check your worksheet.

Here's an excerpt of what a daily worksheet might look like while you are chasing your dream. Remember that this is the daily worksheet that focuses on your dream only.

FERNANDO L. SOTO

DAILY WORKSHEET		Date: April 2
High Priority (20%/80% Results)	**Business Tasks**	
1 Read Chap 4, Rules for Renegades	1 Meet with James about networking	
2 Attend Orientation meeting at college	2 Work on business plan	
3 Register for business class	3 Get demographics information at library	
4 Finish reading Napoleon Hill	4	
5 Order CD for car: Malcolm Gladwell's new book	5	
6	6	
7	7	
8	8	
9	9	
10	10	
Personal Tasks	11	
1 Mail taxes.	12	
2 Send Joann a birthday card (5/5)	13	
3	14	
4	15	
Appointments		
5:30AM Check Daily Worksheet	2:00PM	
6:00AM Read Napoleon Hill	2:30PM	
6:30AM	3:00PM Check Daily Worksheet	
7:00AM	3:30PM	
7:30AM	4:00PM	
8:00AM	4:30PM	
8:30AM	5:00PM Orientation meeting	
9:00AM New client visit, PCS Medical Group	5:30PM	
9:30AM	6:00PM	
10:00AM	6:30PM Check Daily Worksheet	
10:30AM	7:00PM Stop at library	
11:00AM Check Daily Worksheet	7:30PM	
11:30AM	8:00PM	
12:00PM Read Rules for Renegades, Chap. 4	8:30PM	
12:30PM	9:00PM Online business course	
1:00PM	9:30PM	
1:30PM	10:00PM	
Messaging & Notes		

WHAT'S NEXT FOR YOU?

Did you notice that there are not a lot of work-related items that deal with your present job? That's because the main purpose of this worksheet is to focus your attention on the things that need to be done to achieve your dream. Look at the second daily worksheet on the next page. That's what it might look like once you are living your dream.

As you can see, there are many more things to do once you start living your dream. Just remember the difference between the two worksheets and don't lose sight of their separate and individual purposes. The Daily Worksheet for your dream should only concentrate on and record your goals and activities that are dream-related (aside from the few personal things that you need to remember to do.) The second worksheet should concentrate on all the things you need to do to maintain your dream while you are living it. Because mine was to run my own business, I used that as an example. Your worksheet will look the way you need it to look because you will need it to work for you and always remember that education, inspiration and motivation will always be important components of how you spend your days. The idea here is to keep growing and moving forward. You will constantly need to evaluate and re-evaluate what you do each day. Never lose sight of how important that is. Your daily worksheets will help you with that.

I know people who are really good at remembering to write down all of the events they have coming up on a calendar or daily planner. The only thing is…they forget to check them. This is important because a few days may go by, taking a few events with them. A calendar only works if you check it. Just like your new daily worksheet. If you make a point to check your worksheet in the morning and again at the end of your day – and for some of us, multiple times throughout the day – it will become habit and whether things in your life pile up or not, you will check it. That's because habits are behavior routines, like brushing your teeth or checking the mail. You always do those things,

FERNANDO L. SOTO

DAILY WORKSHEET		Date: April 2
HighPriority(20%/80%Results)	**BusinessTasks**	
1 Read Chap 12, Galdwell book	1 Meet with Pat about networking	
2 Employee evaluations: Jon, Sara, Michael, Tom, Nikki	2 Evaluate business plan	
3 Register for business class	3 Place ad online for two new openings	
4 New client goal: 5 by end of the week	4 Go over payroll with Margie	
5 Order CD for car	5	
6 Hire two new people	6	
7	7	
8	8	
9	9	
10	10	
PersonalTasks	11	
1 Pick up kids from school	12	
2 Send Mark a birthday card (birthday is June 4)	13	
3 Shop for anniversary gift	14	
4	15	
Appointments		
5:30AM Check Daily Worksheet	2:00PM Employee evaluation: Jonathon S.	
6:00AM Read Napoleon Hill	2:30PM Employee evaluation: Sara M.	
6:30AM	3:00PM Check Daily Worksheet	
7:00AM	3:30PM Employee evaluation: Tom	
7:30AM	4:00PM Employee evaluation: Nikki	
8:00AM Breakfast update meeting	4:30PM Plant tour: new client at Jonestown	
8:30AM Pat in conference room	5:00PM	
9:00AM New client visit: JRP Legal Group	5:30PM Employee evaluation: Michael	
9:30AM	6:00PM Pick up kids	
10:00AM New client call: Morris & Morris	6:30PM Check Daily Worksheet	
10:30AM New client call: CRRM Medical Group	7:00PM Stop at library	
11:00AM Check Daily Worksheet	7:30PM	
11:30AM Payroll meeting with Margie	8:00PM	
12:00PM Read Rules for Renegades, Chap. 4/Lunch	8:30PM	
12:30PM New client visit: Optical Illusions, Inc	9:00PM Online business course	
1:00PM	9:30PM	
1:30PM New client call: Ben Mapes	10:00PM	
Messaging & Notes		
What's next for you? 20/80		

WHAT'S NEXT FOR YOU?

right? They're habits. Make checking your daily worksheet a habit. That way it becomes a part of your daily routine. That's how you will get closer to your dream, day-by-day.

> **"Make checking your daily worksheet a habit.**
> **That way it becomes a part of your daily routine.**
> **That's how you will get closer to your dream, day-by-day."**

We are all human and human beings sometimes put things off. But remember this: From now on, you are not allowed to do that. You are not allowed to forget to check your daily worksheet. You are not allowed to skip out on the time you set aside to work on your dream. No playing hookey. No procrastinating…and for many people, procrastination is a very real struggle.

By definition, procrastination means to put off or delay doing something that needs immediate attention. It means finding other ways to occupy your time instead of doing the things you need to do. Procrastination is an art form for some people and by that I don't mean a process yielding a creative product. I mean that procrastination is more of a process that uses creativity as excuses not to get things done. It is a way to avoid being successful. Now, if you are a procrastinator, faithfully checking your worksheet may be difficult. Remember I said earlier that chasing your dream is not for the faint of heart? Here is one example of where things may get tough for some of us. This is where you must be sure to stay the course. Check your worksheet. Stay on track…and then check your worksheet again, because checking your worksheet will really help you do the things you need to do.

Let's use your brother's birthday as an example here. When you are devoted to and rely on your worksheet, you will begin to notice that as you get closer and closer to your brother's birthday, the task of physically going out and purchasing a birthday card, writing a note and signing it, licking the envelope and sticking on a stamp and mailing it moves higher and higher up the sheet until the job makes its way to the "High Priority" column. If you earnestly and honestly follow and use your worksheet religiously, the task of sending a birthday card to your brother will get done before it reaches the number one spot in the high priority column.

Think about a typical day. Every minute of every day we are bombarded with advertisements, find ourselves in stressful situations, deal with all kinds of issues, get hungry, tired, sick and distracted. We cannot rely on memory. We need help. That's what my Daily Worksheet is for: To help you remember that you are working on something significant; something that means something to you; something that will bring a huge amount of positive change into your life one day.

Chasing your dream:

Here's how it works. Perform the "High Priority" items first. Then address the business tasks and then the personal ones. Only write down the really important dream-related appointments in the "Appointments" section. Never ever forget this: You are chasing your dream and it is the most important thing. It's high priority. As a result, one worksheet should be dedicated to your dream only. If you want to keep another worksheet for all of your other personal appointments and affairs, that's fine. But you must have one that keeps track of your dream and you must follow it.

You must follow it for this to work.

Let's make another sign. You should already have a few index cards taped in places that you can see each day. Here's another one. On an index card, write 80/20.

Like this:

80/20

This card is going to remind you of the 80/20 Principle. The 80/20 Principle is simple. It means that 20% of your efforts should bring you 80% of your results. It is based on Vilfredo Federico Damaso Pareto's principle of imbalance. Pareto (1848-1923) was a French-born Italian engineer. He did a lot of work with welfare economics and while this principle has never been proven as scientific law, it goes something like this: Most of a result (80%) is due to

WHAT'S NEXT FOR YOU?

20% of factors. For example, the Pareto Principle states that 80% of sales may be attributed to 20% of customers. [30] I use the card and it reminds me not to waste too much time with the things that aren't going to yield me results. This principle applies when your dream is up and running.

Right now your time is precious. You have analyzed it, scheduled it, and now you need to prioritize it. Don't waste 80 percent of your time on things that will only move you 20 percent of the way. If you start reading something and find that it is not what you need, put it down and find another book. Carefully decide what you will do with your time. It is so important to keep your eye on that dream. Invest your time wisely. That's how you will see results and remember...the 80/20 Principle means that 20 percent of your efforts should bring you 80 percent of your results, not the other way around. If not, then you are working too hard.

I am a firm believer in using your time wisely. Both my Personal Timesheet and Daily Worksheet attest to that. Getting closer to achieving your goals and living your dream means putting every minute you have into the pursuit. You must be motivated and consistent. You must be ruthless and relentless and so even when I have a few minutes, I can find something useful to do. In fact, I always have something on deck to do. I can read a few pages in a great business book or talk to a supportive coworker about my dream. I can check my daily worksheet and focus on what I have lined up to do. Or I can check my daily worksheet and work on chipping away at the least important things.

Close your eyes and picture a mouse on one of those wheels. The mouse is running, running, running, and yet is still in the same place he started. That's how I felt before I focused and started working to chase my dream. Thanks to procrastination and a host of other reasons why we don't get as much accomplished each day as we can, I would work all day and get nowhere. I did that for many years. My Daily Worksheet will help you be more productive. It helped me. But remember, it will only work, if you use it. You have to look at it every morning and prepare a new one every night before you go to bed and everything you say you plan to do, you need to do. You actually have to follow through with what you set yourself up to do. What I am basically asking you to do is create a new habit. Something that you learn to do that you are not used to doing right now; something that becomes a habit.

Habits are not born overnight. It takes motivation to change the way you are doing something now and start doing it in an entirely new way. It also takes commitment to keep that new habit going. Here are some helpful hints that may help:

1. **Commit to one month**. The experts tell us that creating a new habit takes at least 21 days of consistently doing something new to make it automatic. Of course, getting into the habit of checking your daily worksheet is something you will be doing for a very long time. It is worthwhile to invest the time and energy into making this important activity one of your daily habits.
2. **Remind yourself**. Find little ways to remember to check your daily worksheet. Even though at this point, you are already thinking about your dream almost all the time, there may be times when you might forget to check in with your daily worksheet. In other words, it may not be automatic in the beginning. Post it notes are great. Write a reminder to yourself on one and stick it on your nightstand where you will see it when you wake up. Or attach one to the bathroom mirror or coffee maker. Wherever you know you will be in the morning. Before you know it, checking in with your daily worksheet will be another habit.
3. **Be consistent**. Schedule times when you plan and check your worksheet. By making it the same time each day, you will be helping it to become second nature and it will eventually become habit.
4. **Use a trigger activity**. A trigger activity is something you do right before you do the habit you want to form. For example, you might make a pot of coffee and pour yourself a cup right before you settle in to devote a scheduled hour to reading or listening to a motivational or inspirational business book. Or you might shower and then sit down with the newspaper and your daily worksheet. A trigger activity is just that, it uses an already established habit to trigger and ultimately reinforce another activity.

WHAT'S NEXT FOR YOU?

5. **Replenish the things you remove.** If you are giving up relaxation time in front of the television, replace it with a relaxing hour of reading something that will fuel your dream. In other words, don't deprive yourself of that patch of quiet time. By switching in an activity that is close to the type of activity you were doing, you will not only be getting your relaxation time in, but you will also be moving closer to the life you dream.
6. **Write down your goal.** This one I hope you've already done. It's a good example of an important activity that can be written on your daily worksheet. If you want to read a business book from 7 to 8 p.m., make sure you write it down.

An unknown author once wrote: "Ordinary people think merely of spending time. Great people think of using it." Lee Iacocca, author, advocate, and American business executive at Ford Motor Company and then, later, at Chrysler Corporation, wisely said: "If you want to make good use of your time, you've got to know what's most important and then give it all you've got."

Don't waste time. Give your dream and your life the time and attention it deserves.

Give yourself the attention you deserve.

Chapter Twelve
FOUR KEY TRUTHS

"Never, never, never, never give up."
- Winston Churchill

Now is as good a time as any to spend a few pages reviewing and reiterating. When we are in school, teachers do that all the time so that we don't forget what we learned. It never hurts to go back to the beginning and remember why we're here in the first place.

We are here because we want to leap out of bed, race out the door, and get to work because it is the most challenging and awesome thing we ever wanted to do. We are here because we want our work life to be more than just work. We are here because of the dream.

Your dream.

You are here because you know that if you believe in it, your dream will come true. You asked yourself what was next for you and answered. You read the sidebars and pullout quotes. You answered the questions and filled in the blanks. You are here because you believe in yourself.

You know you can eek out the time you need to do the things that have to be done to live the life you can't imagine not living. So, congratulations. Great job! You are the ones who didn't put the book down. You kept coming back to hear how I did it. You kept reading because you want to do it, too and you are still here because you know I can help get you there.

Notice I didn't say I could get you there? That's because this is all on you. I can give you suggestions, hints, time management tips, charts, worksheets, inspirational quotes and a reading list. I can tell you what the experts say and do and tell you stories about real people I know, but you are the one who will actually do the work. You are the one who needs to be motivated enough to go through this adventure. You need to be as motivated as my friend.

I know a woman who let absolutely nothing get in the way of her dream. She recently became a licensed barber after graduating from cosmetology school. Her perfect attendance, positive attitude and leadership skills earned her accolades and monetary bonuses. For two years she got out of bed, left her house and went to school. She signed up for her classes knowing that getting there every day would be challenging without a car and driver's license, but it didn't matter to her- taxi, bicycle, car pool, bus. She wasn't exactly sure how she was going to get there. She just knew she would get there. She just knew she would…

…and she did.

This woman made a commitment to herself to go back to school. Her lack of transportation was not going to be a factor to her anymore. She decided there were going to be no more excuses and she was going to put what she always wanted to do front and center. One way or the other, she was determined to go back to school and get her degree. She was determined to live her dream and as we have seen in other stories of people who put their dreams before all else, this woman's dream became her obsession. Nothing got in the way. She achieved what she had always wanted to do in life, just like the ASE Certified Automotive Technician. She achieved her dream.

I achieved my dream, too and you will achieve yours.

This woman has high spirits and great wisdom. Her attitude resembles her accomplishments. Ask her, and she would be proud to tell you about the many ladders she's had to climb and obstacles she's had to overcome to get to where she is today…and while she is willing to share how she pushed through the challenges, she is also happy to talk about how she felt at her graduation ceremony. Today, this woman is motivated to continue doing the best she can do. She is living her dream and will keep moving forward. That's because she is positive and full of life and energy. Like a plant that's been nurtured, this woman is bright, vibrant, rich in color and moist. There's no dry and falling apart here. Oh, and one more thing: This woman is 64 years old.

I know, huh?

My friend and her story is a perfect example of how chasing your dream makes you more alive. At 64 years old, she is living life to the fullest. She is attractive and a wonderful and wise resource to the people around her.

Doesn't that sound exciting?

As you continue to move forward and closer to living your dream, you will feel more and more alive. The challenges will still be there, but your attitude will enable you to overcome them. I hope you are reading lots of books by successful businessmen and women and I know if you are, you are seeing many examples of how success is synonymous with a positive attitude, an open mind and a motivated spirit. Like me, I hope you are being challenged in thought and feel moved to get busy. I learned so much from the advice and words of wisdom of many, many people in the books I read and listened to. If you are faithfully reading and paying attention, you will, too and now, here are four truths I have learned by reading, listening and living. You need to know them, too.

"As you continue to move forward and closer to living your dream, you will feel more and more alive. The challenges will still be there, but your attitude will enable you to overcome them."

1. Not chasing your dream will diminish who you are.

There. I said it and believe me, it's true. Not chasing your dream will strip you of your self-esteem and your true identity. You will begin to feel left out of life and left behind. It will happen slowly and it will happen over time, but it will happen and here's why.

WHAT'S NEXT FOR YOU?

Let's face it. When you are not doing what you really want to do, you get sad. This feeling of sadness can pop up anywhere. It can overcome you as you argue or debate with someone and find that you cannot make your point. It can pop up when you can't afford the really nice pair of shoes you want. It's there when you are playing a game or a sport and want to win, but you don't. Over time, this feeling of sadness turns into discouragement. You begin to feel like you've never accomplished anything. You feel like a "loser." When you aren't doing the things you really want to do, your frame of mind changes and once the sadness changes to discouragement, everything else changes, too. Your character, your outlook on life and your personality begin to get in your way. As you move forward, you find that your opportunities are limited and you find that you are not really moving forward at all. This can happen not only when it comes to debating with others, buying shoes, or winning a sporting event, but it can happen to you when you are not following your dream. It's exactly the same because your dream defines your future. If you convince yourself that you don't have a future, then you will most likely give up hope. Eventually, without hope, you may begin to feel empty. This leads to a loss of confidence in yourself. You don't believe you can live your dream. As a result, you give up all together. You end up accepting things the way they are and living day-to-day, allowing circumstances to push you around.

Always remember: You are the one in charge of your future. Like Napoleon Hill says, "Whatever the mind can conceive and believe, you can achieve." Don't train yourself to quit.

2. People who follow their dreams are creators.
Dream chasers create the world we will live in tomorrow. They are the politicians, artists, musicians, performers, businessmen and entrepreneurs. They can be you, too. It was President John F. Kennedy's dream for Americans to go to the moon. In his historic speech on May 25, 1961, Kennedy spoke about safely sending humans to the Moon by the end of the decade. Then, on July 20, 1969, Apollo 11 astronaut Neil Armstrong stepped down off the ladder of the Lunar Module onto the bumpy, dusty surface of the Moon. Within minutes,

he and fellow astronaut Edwin "Buzz" Aldrin walked around for three hours. They collected small pieces of moon rocks and dirt. They did some experiments. They left a sign and planted an American flag. It took less than 10 years for President Kennedy's dream to come true, but that's how big dreams begin.

Think about it...internet, high speed everything, electrical devices, name brand products, better roads and bridges, gadgets galore, toys, septic systems, communities. There are a lot of thinkers out there, but...the ones who translate that thinking into action are the ones who are benefiting from the pursuit of their vision. These are the people who change the world.

Wouldn't you like to be someone who changes the world? Wouldn't you like to create a product, invent something, help someone, or sing, dance, or work for a good cause? It's simple. Change your dream.

Create.

In our society, the most influential people are the dream chasers. They are the ones we watch and follow. They are the ones who refuse to put their dreams on hold. They were not afraid to pursue. They wanted to do something with their lives and as they chased after that dream, they slowly changed the world they live in.

They changed the world we live in.

3. Pursuing your dream will empower you. It will make you stronger.

Chasing after a dream is not easy work. The chase toward accomplishment will throw you around a little. It will beat you up. It will upset you, confuse you, stress you out, scare you and make you nervous, but it will also give you the ride of your life. It will force you to break new ground. It will keep the boring out while providing zero comfort zones. As terrifying as all of that sounds, you must stay true to your dream; as exhilarating as all of that sounds, you must stay true to your dream. You must.

Think of someone you know who is strong. Choose someone who is not physically strong, but emotionally, mentally, or spiritually strong. Watch the way they conduct themselves. Do they seem more confident? Are they more independent? Do they do what they are supposed to do? Are they committed?

WHAT'S NEXT FOR YOU?

Are they proud? Well, I bet you answered yes to most, if not all, of those questions. Strong people are more confident and independent. They do what they are supposed to do and are both committed and proud, but sometimes, even strong people can have a setback or two.

Take David Neeleman, for example. Neeleman recognized how airline travel had become increasingly more and more unpleasant and less customer-focused. This resulted in expensive flights that were cramped and slow. People felt they were being treated rudely by airline personnel and there were no other options. Neeleman looked at the whole picture and realized that airline travel is more about customer service than anything else. As a result, he started an airline that everyone called "people-friendly." As JetBlue founder and chief executive officer, Neeleman successfully followed his dream and created an airline where people finally felt appreciated. He left no stone unturned as he worked to pursue and achieve his vision of what air travel should be like. Then, in 2007, after a series of delays and cancellations because of the weather, Neeleman was asked to step down as CEO. This was a huge setback for someone who has such a love of both airplanes and customer service. His vision really did make a difference. So, instead of running away, Neeleman turned toward home. Born in Brazil, he saw an opportunity and chased it down. He began scouting out opportunities in this fast-growing country and raised almost $240 million to start a new airline. He even invested $13 million of his own money to get Azul Airlines off the ground. Just a year after JetBlue let him go, Azul started flying people around Brazil. As of this writing, he is still CEO of Azul and spends his spare time working to raise money for and recognize young people with learning disabilities and attention deficit disorder. [31]

Neeleman did not let a big setback stop him from living his dream.

Setbacks are tough and you will learn more about how to deal with them in a later chapter, but they have the potential to make us stronger. Sometimes a few steps back help put things into perspective. It gives you a chance to analyze and look forward. It really is true what people say about challenges. The things that we face that don't kill us really do make us stronger.

4. Chasing your dream will educate you.

For me, the pursuit to own a business was an opportunity to learn about many things. I had a real-life, crash course in business. I became educated in accounting, staff management, organizational leadership, human resources, sales, marketing, telemarketing, payroll, record keeping, contracts and agreements, and laws pertaining to employment, business issues, and trademarks. The educational benefits didn't stop there, though. The more I chased my dream, the more I learned about being a better father, spouse, son, and brother. I learned how to give back and value the simple things in life that don't cost any money, like relationships and personal experiences. I matured. I stood up straighter. I began to respect people. Chasing my dream forced me to really think. Chasing your dream will make you think, too and as a result, you will learn lots of new stuff. It will broaden your horizons and change your perspective about many things. Chasing your dream will make you smarter. You're going to be prouder.

More Key Truths

Here are some takeaways from this chapter…plus a few more truths I learned while chasing my dream:

- You're the only one in control of your future.
- Chasing your dream will make you a better person.
- Chasing your dream will make you stronger, smarter and more attractive.
- If you fail or experience a setback, you are not alone. Just get back up and get going.
- If living your dream was easy, everyone would be doing it.

Just remember my 64-year-old friend. She finally followed her dream and now she can walk into any barber shop and know what's going on. She knows all about the clips, clippers, combs, shaving cream, licensing and the different haircut styles. She has learned to deal with landlords, lenders and the finances and legalities of her field. She understands the lingo. She is stronger and smarter for having achieved her dream.

WHAT'S NEXT FOR YOU?

Keep on chasing your dream and always remember that living your dream means rolling up your sleeves and getting to work. You may fail a few times, but getting back up and trying again will make all the difference in your world. In the end, you will come out stronger, more intelligent and with much more wisdom and real-life, beneficial experiences. Just stick with it and never, never, NEVER give up.

Chapter Thirteen
NAYSAYERS AND SETBACKS

> *"It's easy to have faith in yourself and have discipline when you're a winner, when you're number one. What you got to have is faith and discipline when you're not a winner."*
>
> - VINCE LOMBARDI

Naysayers. Setbacks. Stuff. We all have all three. It's how we learn to deal with and handle each situation that makes the difference. In chasing your dream, I can guarantee you will come into contact with all three at some point. The challenges that you face as you move forward will be both rewarding and daunting. The rewarding ones will be easy. It's the daunting lessons that will be much more difficult to work through.

If you tried to pursue your dream before and failed, you're not alone. Everybody fails at something at some point in their lives. It's like that old saying about getting up more times than the number of times you fall down. Always remember that if living your dream was easy, everyone would be doing it and the reality is that everyone is not living their dream. That means that it's going to be hard work. Yes, I've said that many, many times already. I just want you to be ready to fall down a few times, at least and then have the ability and motivation to pull yourself back up. Not an easy feat with all those naysayers, setbacks, and stuff.

By definition, a naysayer is "a person who habitually expresses negative or pessimistic views." Basically, a naysayer is a person with a very bad attitude who is not afraid to parade it around. In fact, a naysayer will aggressively rain on your parade every chance he or she gets. Naysayers complain a lot and always look at the worst case scenario of any situation. They can rant and whine and banter negatively for hours. They drain your battery and suck the life right out of you. The Urban Dictionary states that naysayers tend to "blend in with those around them rather well." So they look like everyone else, until they open their mouths and show their true colors. These are people that can only do you harm and while the Urban Dictionary describes naysayers at length, they offer a little hope by acknowledging the non-naysayer. According to the dictionary, a non-naysayer is someone who fights against negativity and stands up against naysayers.

Be a Non-Naysayer.

The reality is that we all have a naysayer or two in our lives. For one reason or another, this particular negative individual does not want to see us succeed. Sometimes you can win a naysayer over from the dark side, but more often than not, it's best to turn a deaf ear or walk away from the relationship, if that's possible. Sometimes it is and sometimes it isn't.

Another thing about naysayers is that they disguise themselves as experts and as you know, there are plenty of experts running around. The difference between a naysayer and an expert, though, is their view of life. While an expert has lots of skill or knowledge about a certain subject, a naysayer only goes by what he or she hears about a topic and how he or she feels about it. As I said earlier, naysayers are aggressively negative about the subjects they feel strongly about. The funny thing is, they are most often wrong. For example, in 1899, Charles H. Duell, the commissioner of the U.S. Office of Patents, reiterated an older quote by saying, "Everything that can be invented has been invented."

Naysayer.

In 1962, an executive from the Decca Recording Company rejected the Beatles as a client, saying, "We don't like their sound, and guitar music is on the way out." [32]

Wow. Naysayer.

Lord Kelvin, who was president of the Royal Society in 1895 said, "Heavier-than-air flying machines are impossible."

Tell that to David Neeleman.

In response to Fred Smith's paper proposing a way to deliver packages reliably and quickly overnight, his Yale University professor said, "The concept is interesting and well-formed, but in order to earn better than a 'C,' the idea must be feasible."

Fred Smith is the founder of FedEx. [33]

Wow.

One more…

When Debbi Fields' followed her dream to mass-market her wonderful Mrs. Fields' Cookies, one naysayer was quoted as saying: "A cookie store is a bad idea. Besides, the market research reports say America likes crispy cookies, not soft and chewy cookies like you make." [34]

Really?

Thank goodness Debbi Fields did not listen to the naysayers in her life, for if she had, she would not be where she is today. Armed with a recipe and a dream, Debbi was 20 years old when she talked a loan officer at a bank into financing her idea. In August of 1977, she opened Mrs. Fields Chocolate Chippery in Pablo Alto, CA. More than twenty years later, there were 600-plus franchises and company-owned Mrs. Fields' bake shops in America. Her company was worth $450 million before she sold it. Now Debbi Fields is an author and philanthropist.

Debbi Fields had no business training. She was a housewife with a great cookie recipe and a lifelong dream. She was motivated and focused and achieved her goal. Her story is a great example of how naysayers can stand in the way of your success if you let them. [35]

WHAT'S NEXT FOR YOU?

More Famous Naysayers

After more than 20 companies turned down his idea, Chester F. Carlson didn't give up, invented the copy machine and then founded the Xerox Company. [36]

Called the Father of Radio and Grandfather of Television, Dr. Lee DeForest once said: "Man will never reach the moon regardless of all future scientific advances." [37]

"Who the hell wants to hear actors talk?" H.M. Warner of Warner Brothers was quoted saying this in 1927.[38]

Here's Steve Jobs' account of what happened when he and Steve Wozniak pitched their prototype of the personal computer: "So we went to Atari and said, 'Hey, we've got this amazing thing, even built with some of your parts and what do you think about funding us? Or we'll give it to you. We just want to do it. Pay our salary, we'll come work for you.' And they said, 'No.' So then we went to Hewlett-Packard, and they said, 'Hey, we don't need you. You haven't got through college yet.'" [39]

Debbi Fields grew her idea regardless of naysayers. I'm sure she also dealt with setbacks, too. A setback is an unfortunate and frustrating event that thwarts progress. Setbacks come in many shapes and sizes. Henry Ford (1863-1947), American industrialist and founder of the Ford Motor Company, knew all about setbacks. He once said, "Life is a series of experiences, each one of which makes us bigger, even though sometimes it is hard to realize this. For the world was built to develop character, and we must learn that the setbacks and grieves which we endure help us in our marching onward." [40]

I love that.

Ford experienced setbacks and turned them into learning experiences. We can all learn from this. Everything that works against us is an opportunity to grow, whether it is a financial setback, or problems with family or friends. Maybe your car broke down. Maybe you lost your job. There are many examples of unfortunate events that can break a spirit or cause discouragement.

Don't let it.

Setbacks. Crisis. Failure. Call it whatever you will, but remember that setbacks are just that. They temporarily push you away from your goal. The important thing to do when experiencing a setback is confront it and take it on. Don't let it take you on. Look at setbacks as opportunities to grow stronger and smarter. Keep your eye on your dream and you will overcome your setback. You can also try a few of these tactics.

"Look at setbacks as opportunities to grow stronger and smarter."

Believe in yourself. That's right. You, because in the end, it's your life and as long as your dream is front and center and you are focused and motivated, you will live it through.

Talk to someone. Maybe you have a friend who has been supportive from the beginning or know a co-worker or boss you can trust. Talking to someone who has overcome setbacks themselves is a good way to help you overcome the same.

Be positive. I can't say this enough times. That's because it's so important to stay positive and upbeat.

Go back and reread the cards. Remember the index cards all around your house and in your car? Read them again. Recite them. Remember them.

Review. Go back over your timesheets to appreciate yourself and how much work and time and effort you are putting in to achieve your dream. Maybe add another daily worksheet to monitor your progress more closely. Reread a few chapters in this book. Whatever you decide to do, make sure it's positive and nurturing and something that will get you to stay on track in spite of the setback.

Throughout history, there are thousands of examples of setbacks in business. Did you know that Henry Ford went bankrupt five times? Well, he did and he did that before he became a great success in the automobile industry. Aside from living a long, long time ago, Henry Ford is no different from you or me. This is important, so pay attention. All the books you are reading now that describe successful business practices and ventures are written by men and women just like you. Just like me. None of these people have super powers

or extreme intelligence. Each one found a way within their own worlds to tap into strengths and found resources that helped them achieve success. They all pretty much have the same things in common with you and with me:
1. They know what they want. We do, too.
2. They are confident they can do anything if they put their mind to it. Just like us.
3. They were prepared to fail. After reading this chapter, you will be, too.

Super Setbacks

Really? You think your setback is super? Take a look at these:
- When Thomas Edison was working on inventing the light bulb, he failed about 10,000 times before it worked.
- John Grisham, author of 23 bestselling books, including *The Runaway Jury*, *The Pelican Brief*, and *The Firm*, was rejected by 16 literary agents and 12 publishing houses when he tried to get his first book, *A Time to Kill*, published.[41]
- Film star Harrison Ford, who played memorable characters such as Han Solo in *Star Wars* and Indiana Jones in the Indiana Jones movies, was told early in his career by movie executives that he didn't have what it takes to be a star. Really?
- Before her Harry Potter fame, J.K. Rowling, author, was penniless and depressed. She was writing her first novel while going to school and being a single mother to her child. Talk about setbacks. She started out on welfare and is now one of the richest women in the world and it only took five years! She's a billionaire.

So there are naysayers and setbacks, but what about all the other stuff?

By stuff I mean health issues, childcare problems and all of the other day-to-day, minute-to-minute things we all have to deal with. Your stuff is what you have. They're the things you carry around with you. You can see some of your stuff and some of your stuff you can't see. It's important and it affects us in different ways and again, it's all in how we deal with things.

When I think of stuff, I think of people who have overcome life's little frustrating surprises with grace and common sense. I think this is such a personal topic because even though saying we all have stuff is a universal truth, all of our stuff is not the same. I want you to do something right now. Close your eyes and take a few slow, deep breaths. Is there something going on in your life right now that was not expected? Something that maybe blindsided you? Maybe your teenager crashed your only car and thank Goodness no one was hurt, but now you have no way to get to work. Maybe you got sick and missed a week at work. Living paycheck to paycheck, that loss translates into missed payments or bills that couldn't be covered. Write it here. Right now.

_____

_____

_____

_____

Okay. Now…how do you deal with things? How do you handle the stuff that life throws at you? Is it faith in God that helps get you through? Is it a support system of friends, coworkers or your spouse? Write a few words describing how you get through stuff here.

_____

_____

_____

_____

WHAT'S NEXT FOR YOU?

Reread what you wrote up there. This is important because when your energy and resources are going toward chasing your dream and suddenly your life is turned upside down by stuff, sticking to your daily plan may be challenging. This is what I was talking about in Chapter 12. Pursuing your dream will get tough. Sometimes all of the stuff really makes it hard to keep going. Use your support system. Talk to people and sometimes it even helps to remember that we learn more from the hard stuff than the easy stuff.

Believe it or not, there are tons of blogs on the Internet that deal with stuff. I found many, many great blogs addressing how to stay focused, how to overcome adversity and how to learn from mistakes. Many are written by entrepreneurs or business leaders or even people like you and me who are chasing our dreams. Look them up. They are worth a read.

Like novels and movies, blogs are personal and not everyone likes the same kinds of things. Really…go find five or ten to follow every day. You never know what kind of useful information or motivational stories will touch you and your day.

Bottom line: everyone has stuff. It's what we do with that stuff, with the setbacks and with the naysayers that make or break us. You are working so hard at pursuing your dream, staying motivated and using your time so wisely. It's important not to lose your momentum and while I'm not saying to ignore everything around you, what I am saying is to try to stay focused.

Don't lose sight of where you are going.

Chapter Fourteen
WHY PERSISTENCE AND CONSISTENCY COUNT

"The best way to predict the future is to create it."
- PETER DRUCKER (1909-2005), WRITER,
MANAGEMENT CONSULTANT, BUSINESS THINKER

Remember that busy Saturday afternoon when you had tons of errands to run and your car wouldn't start? You were parked in a large, crowded parking lot and with arms filled with shopping bags, you headed out of the mall and toward your car. You unlock your trunk and put the packages in. You're thinking ahead. You are mentally checking things off your large list of things to do today and planning your next stop. You unlock your car door and climb inside. Key goes into the ignition and...click. Click. Click. Nothing.

Dead.

It's not out of gasoline, because then the car would still have some life. There would be lights and the radio would work. There would be power windows and a funny growling sound when you turned the key in the ignition. Today, however, you are getting nothing at all. It's your battery and it's dead and without the battery, the car will not start. It will not take you to the next stop on your list or to your friend's house. It leaves your car in a frozen state of going nowhere. You can change the windshield wipers, get new tires and even fill the tank with gasoline, but if the battery is dead, that car is going nowhere.

In chapter two, your dream was the battery that kept your engine going. You could have sat there in your car and done nothing at all, but then you wouldn't have gotten this far. You pulled yourself together, evaluated the situation, and got yourself a new battery.

Well, you are probably still driving that same car. But since that parking lot incident, you have gotten an oil change, a tune-up, new tires and an alignment. You know that if you take good care of your car, it will do what you need it to do. To me, when things are working, it's like a well-oiled machine, or car. It runs smoothly. All the parts are working at their optimum levels and as a result, you are getting to where you need to go. In the pursuit and journey to reach your dreams, you should be driving a well-oiled, well-greased, well-maintained vehicle and if you keep your car on a regular maintenance schedule and take care of small problems before they become big ones, you will have a reliable way to get to where you want to be.

Get it?

There will always be flat tires, dead batteries, and worn-out windshield wipers. Life is not ideal. If it were, there would be no need for mechanics. In an ideal life, you would have no problems and everything would work well and in your favor. You would always be happy and fulfilled. You would have no worries. But lets face it. This is the real world and far from ideal. In this chapter, I will help you build the path toward your dream life.

It's all about consistency.

In your hands, you have the power to build a successful life, one step at a time. Success is built on the little things that you learn to perform consistently for a certain amount of time. Take a good look at your life right now. Most people have tons of things that upset them. Most likely, you do too. You have a family. You are in a relationship. You have a job. There are things you want to do. Mixed in and crawling around everything in your life are the imperfections. Wouldn't it be great to be able to eliminate - or at least cut down on - the imperfections and annoyances? Well, it's all about consistently making smart decisions.

> **"Success is built on the little things that you learn to perform consistently for a certain amount of time."**

Your success is going to be determined by how well you can juggle everything in your life. Decisions must be made. Some things will have to go. Some things will need to be worked on. The decisions you need to make to change things in your life are not easy decisions to make, but, they are decisions that will put you and keep you, on the path toward success. Think of it as having an action figure of yourself. You get to move the small figure of you where you need to go. You get to align yourself accordingly and place yourself in places where you will most likely end up winning the game. You call the shots. You get to make the moves. Each decision is a step toward being in a place that will get you closer and closer to your dream.

No decision is too small.

With that in mind, remember that the end result will outweigh some of the more difficult choices and decisions you may have to make on your way to success. Also, keep in mind that for every success story out there, smart and brave decisions made them a reality. Many successful businesses have had a rocky start and a lot of tough decisions had to be made.

The definition of failure is not trying. It's not getting back up when you get knocked down. Shaking off failure is a decision. Getting back on your feet is a decision. Starting over is a decision. So is making the time to read and study. So is ignoring the naysayers and devoting every single second of your life to your dream. Whether it's a new business, a new hobby, a lavish garden, a dance lesson or a creative cooking class, each one of these decisions you must consciously make, one after another, over and over again.

When you have harmonious relationships in your life, when you have steered clear of and kept the naysayers in your life at bay, and when you are

WHAT'S NEXT FOR YOU?

using your time wisely, you will find consistency. It takes hard work, but you will find it. It takes dedication and concentration, but you will learn to be consistent. When I was working as a machine operator while chasing my dream, I would set my machine so well that it would run continuously for hours without tripping up. Sometimes it would operate so effectively that it would not break down during an entire shift. This ability took practice and hard work, but it paid off. I was able to contribute more to the company. I became a valuable resource because of my ability to keep that machine running so effectively and the more efficient and the longer that machine ran without any problems, the more pieces per hour my employer was able to produce.

Think of yourself as that machine.

The definition of consistency is adhering to the same principles, course, or patterns of behavior. Consistency is reliability, uniformity, evenness, steadiness. It is stability. It is regular and all of those things are dependable and unswerving. Unfailing.

Who doesn't want to be called unfailing?

Well, that's what being consistent in thoughts and actions will do for you. The laser-light focus you shine on your dream will pay off. Being consistent will pay off. Now I want you to do something that will help you on your pathway to consistency.

I want you to write your dream in the center circle of the graphic organizer below. It can be one word, a phrase, or a sentence. Describe what it is you are chasing.

Good.

Now look at the three boxes pointing toward your dream. This is where you get to write three things/choices/decisions that you know you will have to consistently make each and every day until you reach your goal and achieve your dream. The example I am using here is getting a pilot's license. So one choice or decision that could go in one of the boxes might be: Turn off the television and study my flight manual every night for one hour. Now this is definitely an example of something you would do everyday to get to where you want to be. It would be very appropriate to write that in one of the boxes in the graphic organizer and it would have been perfect for the chapter on setting up your daily schedules to make time to complete the activities necessary to live the life you dream of. In this graphic organizer, however, I want you to focus more on strategies. For example, I knew that when I was chasing my dream, one of the problems that threatened my growth were the naysayers at work. I had to come up with a strategy that I could deploy almost automatically when and if I felt someone trying to squelch my dream. My strategy was to stay away or engage the person in a conversation about themselves, to take the heat off me. So in this case, for someone who desperately wants to get his or her pilot's license, a naysayer may list all the dangerous things about flying. A strategy to deal with that could be: Smile and politely find something else you need to do. This will get you away from the naysayer.

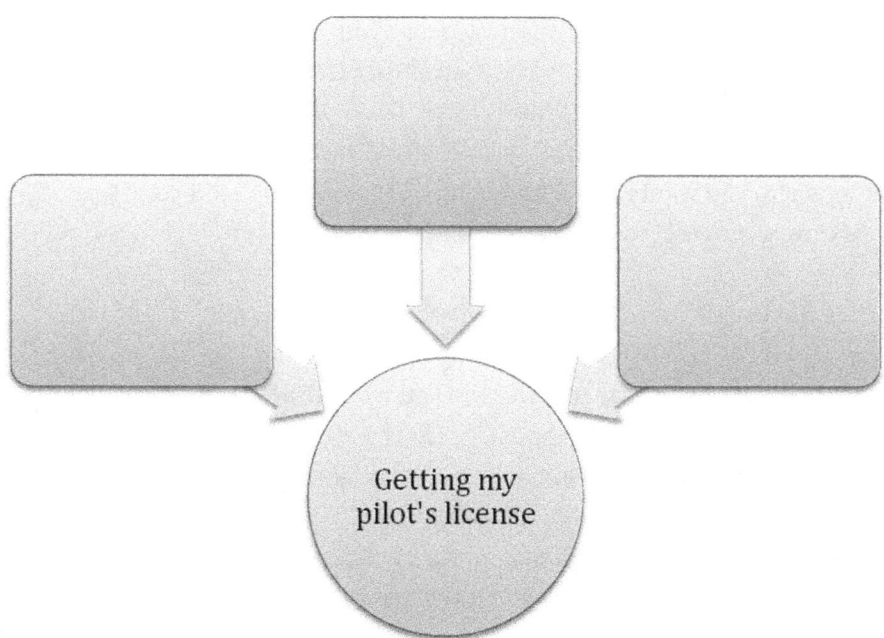

So think of three situations or stumbling blocks you might encounter and then write three of your own strategies in the boxes of the organizer. Here are a few stumbling blocks to get you started.

WHAT'S NEXT FOR YOU?

1. The Internet
2. Television
3. Lack of sleep
4. Fear of failure
5. Fear of success
6. Unhealthy relationships

I'm sure you can think of many more things that can pop up at any time and catch you off guard. The purpose of this exercise – and feel free to repeat as often as you like – is to be ready; to be prepared, because no one really likes to be blindsided.

Take that little action figure of yourself and fight the naysayers. Focus on your dream and fight your problems until they are no longer getting in your way. You have to keep problems away from your life. Keep your eyes on your goal and walk yourself down roads that are free from issues that may steal your attention away from where it needs to be. Don't waste time. Follow your daily schedules and worksheets. You will get there. Just work as hard as you can to get to where you want to be without allowing issues to derail your success.

Because success is what it's all about.

Here's what some more famous people say about success.

1. "Failure is a part of success…Failure will never stand in the way of success if you learn from it." - *Hank Aaron, baseball player*
2. "Everything you want is just outside your comfort zone." – *Robert Allen, author and speaker*
3. "Most of us die with our music unplayed. We should try to step out of our comfort zones and do the things we're capable of." – *Mary Kay Ash (1918-2001), American businesswoman*
4. "Success is a state of mind. If you want success, start thinking of yourself as a success." – *Dr. Joyce Brothers*
5. "Patience, persistence, and perspiration make an unbeatable combination for success." – *Napolean Hill (Yes…we know who he is.)*

6. "You may be disappointed if you fail but you are doomed if you don't try." -- *Beverly Sills, opera singer*
7. "There is no passion to be found playing small – in settling for a life that is less than the one you are capable of living." - *Nelson Mandela, former prime minister of South Africa*
8. "Don't tell me it's impossible." – *Muhammad Ali*

It's so important to never lose sight of where you want to be in life and what you have to do to get there. You are doing great and I know you will succeed. Keep reading. Stay motivated and leap over the pitfalls. You're going to make it. Get ready because in the next chapter, I want to show you my road map to success.

PART THREE

Chapter Fifteen
A ROADMAP FOR SUCCESS

"I like thinking big. If you're going to be thinking anything, you might as well think big."
- Donald Trump

Road maps. You know what they are.

You're planning a trip to somewhere far - somewhere maybe you've never been before – and you go to the corner gas station and pick up the newest, most up-to-date map showing the roads you will take to get to where you are going. You might even pull out a marker or a yellow highlighter and trace along the roads and highways, or route, you plan to take.

Global Positioning Systems. You know what those are, too.

WHAT'S NEXT FOR YOU?

You're planning a trip and you pull out your GPS, plug it into the power source in your car, punch in the destination and a British woman tells you when to "Turn left now. Turn left now." If you take a detour, she also lets you know that she's got you covered. She is recalculating and will have you back on track in seconds.

Either way, you end up where you want to be and when I decided to go after my dream and create a life I would be proud of, I used this same premise. I still do. A road map, for me, is something that I use to follow. It guides me somewhere, and I used one when I was chasing my dream. But instead of a large piece of folded paper or a smallish computerized talking map, I followed people. I looked at the lives of many, many people who did what I wanted to do.

Seriously.

I found learning about others with similar interests and goals as mine to be very enlightening and motivating. Here are a few examples of people who might be interesting to read about. Just remember, any dream, any goal can be accomplished with hard work, determination and motivation. These are just a few examples, and if you don't see what you are interested in here, perform an online search. I'm sure you will find success stories to help you follow your dream.

Here we go…

If you want to start your own business, then read about these famous self-starters.

- Bill Gates, former CEO of Microsoft
- Mary Kay Ash, founder of Mary Kay Cosmetics
- Sam Walton, founder of Walmart and Sam's Club
- Howard Schultz, founder of Starbucks

If you want to run a marathon, read about:

- Wilma Rudolph. As a child, she had polio, scarlet fever, and double pneumonia. She wore a leg brace up until she was 16 years old. She didn't give up her dream, and then in 1956 she won a bronze medal. In 1960 Olympics, Wilma went on to win three gold medals.

If you want to be a chef, read about:
- Guy Fieri. He's a cookbook author and television personality. He co-owns five restaurants and his television show can be seen on Food Network. He credits his father as his greatest inspiration.

If you want to be a writer, read about:
- J.K. Rowling, author of the Harry Potter novels. She was penniless and a single mom. Now, as the result of her hard work and determination, she is one of the richest women in the world.
- Steven King. King was rejected 30 times for his first thriller, *Carrie*. Now King has hundreds of books published and is lauded as one of the best-selling authors of all time.

And if you want to learn about antiques and what they are worth, read about:
- Mike Wolfe. He starting picking through old barns and basements as a young boy and now owns a business called Antique Archaeology. He appears on the History Channel's American Pickers, a television show about Wolfe and his childhood friend, Frank Fritz.

The bottom line…decide what you want and find someone who has done it successfully. Then research, study and learn.

Like I said before, reading about people who were successful at what I wanted to be successful at was helpful, but it was not enough for me. I took it to the next level. I went deeper. I started with a list of entrepreneurs doing what I dreamed of doing and then narrowed it down to the ones who grew up and had a childhood similar to mine, or the ones who came from similar environments as me. Reading the success stories of these business owners and CEOs helped me believe even more that I could achieve my dream. I saw that they went through a lot of the same things that I was going through. I learned how they motivated themselves and overcame their obstacles. Doing this was enlightening and really helped me move forward because these people had gone through a lot of what I was going through. If someone with the same setbacks as me could achieve their dreams, then so could I. I believed that and I am telling you this because I still believe it.

WHAT'S NEXT FOR YOU?

It really works.

I read about the entrepreneurs I had chosen and paid close attention. I followed and implemented much of what they did and said. People like Sam Walton, who opened the very first Walmart in Rogers, Arkansas in 1962, and Napoleon Hill were my inspirations. They both came from the bottom of our economic ladder and climbed to the top. I learned that both Walton and Hill rose to the height of their accomplishments by being consistent and working hard at the right things. Neither one of them wasted time. They valued time. They both demonstrated to me that it doesn't matter where you start out in life.

You should find people who have done what you want to do. Go out and find your role models.

> **"You should find people who have done what you want to do. Go out and find your role models."**

Walton and Hill

I mentioned both Sam Walton and Napoleon Hill in this book because I respect what they have done. They have helped me achieve success.

Here are a few things you might not know about them, though:

* ★ Sam Walton was 44 years old when he opened that very first Walmart store.[42]
* ★ It has been said that Napoleon Hill motivated and influenced more people to live their dreams and become success stories than any other person throughout history.
* ★ After serving in the U.S. Army Intelligence Corps as a captain (1942-1945), Sam Walton got his first job in retail. He worked at a JC Penney store in Iowa. [43]
* ★ Not too long after his mother died, Napoleon Hill became a rebellious teenager.

* Napoleon Hill started writing when he was 13 years old. His first job was as a reporter for his small town newspaper. He became a successful journalist, and then an attorney. [44]
* In Spring of 1992, President George Bush awarded Sam Walton the Presidential Medal of Freedom. This medal is the highest honor a private citizen can be awarded in the United States. It was presented to Walton for his entrepreneurial spirit. The citation read: "An American original, Sam Walton embodies the entrepreneurial spirit it epitomizes and the American dream." It also went on to cite examples of Walton's career, such as the scholarships he sponsored for Latin America, and his commitment to faith, hope, and hard work. [45]
* Napoleon Hill's book, *Think and Grow Rich*, is an all-time best-seller in the field of business and motivation. It is still a big seller. Lots of information about his books and life can be found at the Napoleon Hill Foundation's website.

So here's what you should do...

Research and find a role model. Study everything you can about them. As you read and learn, ask yourself these questions:

1. Why did they do what they did?
2. What kind of environment did they grow up in?
3. What kind of setbacks did they overcome?
4. How did they overcome their setbacks?

While going through this process, it's important not to focus too much on the people who have had completely different upbringings as you. It's not wrong to read about success stories that do not parallel your own life and what you know, but for this step in the process of chasing your dream, it's important to identify with someone from similar circumstances as yourself. This is like matching apples to apples. You need to find people with similar experiences. You need to find another apple.

WHAT'S NEXT FOR YOU?

For example, it would not have made sense for me to read and follow a multi-million dollar chemist with a Ph.D. in chemical engineering who graduated from an Ivy League university if that was not the path I wanted to walk on.

And it wasn't and will not make sense for you, either, if that's not what you desire.

If your dream is to be a pop star, following someone who sings exactly like you and in the same style you sing in and expresses herself or himself in the same way you do would make perfect sense, but if that same pop star was born into a wealthy family who could afford to pay for expensive private lessons and education and expensive studio time, what worked for that person may not work for you if you don't have the same resources as that individual. You would do better to follow the star that had a dream and a very determined attitude, not a lot of money. You would learn more from that person's success story.

Think about this. Isn't it thrilling to read about someone who has overcome bullying, especially if you'd been through the same thing yourself? Or isn't it inspiring to read about the woman who escapes domestic violence, gets out of that abusive situation, and goes on to become an advocate for other battered women. That story is inspiring for you to read, especially if you can relate to her experience of abuse and violence. Or maybe you read a story about a person who is learning to walk after being told he or she would never walk again. That's the kind of story that would motivate you if you were in that same situation. Honestly, though, these kinds of beating-the-odds stories are motivating to all of us, aren't they? Reading them will help you build enthusiasm and hope and serve as a cheerleader for your journey, but just remember, right here, right now, you are looking for someone to learn from who has been where you have been and went to where you want to go.

It all goes back to the road map or GPS. You don't leave your home without knowing where you're going, especially when you've never been there before. It's important to have something that illuminates the way and in this case, let's rely on successful people. So here's an exercise for you to work on.

Go out and find five people who are either living a similar dream to yours or have accomplished what you want to accomplish. Read about them. Research their lives. Find out about who they are and where they've been.

Look into their present lives and back to when they were teenagers. Study their lives in these stages:

- Childhood
- Adolescence
- College years
- Young adulthood

Find out what kind of environment they were raised in, their level of education, what they studied. Study all about their growing up years, the problems they faced, and what their first jobs were. Who inspired them? How did they learn to succeed? In this assignment, you will be working to find out everything you possibly can about these people and this is not something that you can expect to finish in a short amount of time. Really dig in and throw yourself into this project. Use some of the time you have set aside to work on your dream for this. It will be well worth it.

Why?

Because these people are where they are now because they did things in a certain way. You need to find your way and you can do that by studying theirs.

You need to find a connection between you and that person- a turning point.

A turning point is the place where a significant change takes place. It's a click. It's a light bulb moment. A turning point is a decisive moment that changes everything. What was the turning point in Sam Walton's life? What was the turning point in Oprah Winfrey's life?

What will be the turning point in your life?

Keep reading about the people you are researching. Maybe their turning point happened when they were 15 years old and working at a certain job. Maybe their turning point didn't happen until they were 50 years old. The actress, Kathryn Joosten, played Mrs. Landingham on the NBC drama, *The WestWing*. She is pretty well-known for that part she played as secretary to the President of the United States, who was played by Martin Sheen. She also had roles on various sitcoms including *Dharma & Greg, Ally McBeal*, and most recently, *Desperate Housewives*. The thing about Kathryn Joosten is that she didn't start her acting career until she was 42 years old. She didn't make it to Hollywood until almost 10 years later and she took her first role on television at the age of 59. She died in June of 2012 at the age of 72 years, with two Emmy awards…proof that she lived out her dreams.

Upon further research into Kathryn's life, we find that even though she didn't realize her dream until she was well into her middle years, her turning point came when she was in her twenties. Kathryn watched as her mother became sick and died of cancer in 1963. Before she passed away, her mother told her that her biggest regret in life was not going after her dream. It was at that moment that Kathryn decided she would someday be an actress.

And while it took years, her life experiences as a psychiatric nurse and wife and mother helped make her the seasoned and well-loved actress she was. Kathryn never forgot her dream and spent hours working on it before making the choice to dive in and go to Hollywood. Her persistence paid off. [46]

Yours will, too.

So while doing your homework, don't overlook the turning point and make sure you find out what caused it. It is important to see how whatever they did at that defining moment changed the course of their life forever. I've seen this with myself and with my own daughter.

My daughter has a dream and she found someone to read about and learn from. She did her homework and chose a role model. During her reading, she learned that she and her role model had a lot in common. He even attended the same college that she was thinking about attending. She also learned that her role model's first job was consistent with his career choice, too. It was in the same field. She connected with him. What happened to her, happened to me. My role models made me feel the same way. By studying her role model, my daughter saw that everything he did for work, starting with his first job at the age of 15 years, was related to his dream. No wasting time there. The important lesson my daughter learned here is that since work takes up so much of our time, it is critical to try and find work that is consistent with what you're trying to do.

This is a great exercise. Try it.

On a sheet of paper, write down the name of your role model at the top. At the bottom of the page, write down where you are today. Make a small box underneath whatever you wrote down at the bottom and in it give a brief description of your situation. For example, 16 years old, no money, my mom drives me around, work at McDonald's. You get the idea.

Now look at the top of the sheet. How much change do you have to implement to see your dream to reality? How much do you have to learn? Underneath your role model's name, write everything you learned about what he or she went through before getting to where he or she is now. Write in full sentences or jot down notes. Whatever works. Just put down everything that matters in your model's journey to the top.

Still with me? You are making a road map. A record of how you will get to where you want to go.

Next, cross off your role model's name and write your own at the top of the page. Look at your name. What is the next step you need to take? Use the information from your timesheets and daily worksheets to help you plan your trip to achieving your dream. Start where you are today. Remember…you already wrote that at the bottom of the piece of paper. Think and plan ahead. Every move you make should be a move closer to the top. Write today's date at the bottom of the page, where you are now. As you build your road map, you will see yourself getting closer and closer to your dream. Write down your steps to getting there. Using your role model's life as a guide, put in the steps you need to take to get to the top.

Some people think setting a goal date is a good idea, but I don't believe in setting a predetermined date for when you'll achieve your success. No one really knows and it's unrealistic to foresee everything that lies ahead. All I know is that you will know when you get there and when you do, you'll know how long it took because all you have to do is look back at the date at the bottom of the page. That's how long it took. Some dreams are achieved sooner. Some take longer.

It took me six years to achieve my dream of self-employment, but I did it. Keep reading. Keep studying and planning. Keep working and stay motivated and no matter how long it takes, when you get there, this will all have been worth it.

I promise.

Chapter Sixteen
WHAT PASSION MEANS TO ME

"There is no greatness without a passion to be great, whether it's the aspiration of an athlete or an artist, a scientist, a parent, or a businessperson."

- ANTHONY ROBBINS

Passion. This two-syllable word brings to mind many different scenarios to many different people. For a winning athlete, passion translates a love of the game into hours of practice and hard work. Cheering fans. A big win. For a dedicated neurosurgeon, passion means hours of rehearsing and operating and then seeing the faces of a patient's family when surgery goes well. For the entrepreneur, passion can be found in long hours and a workplace where employees are excited and willing to go the extra mile.

We've talked about this before. Passion is jumping out of bed in the morning and racing out the door to go to work at a job you love to do. It is leaping up and out into the world to live your dream.

Think of the movie you go to when you need a boost. Maybe it's the final scenes in *Dirty Dancing* when Baby gets out of the corner and up onto the stage proving to everyone, including her estranged-at-the-moment dad, that she is a hero to someone. Maybe it's the movie, *The Pursuit of Happyness*. (And if you haven't seen it yet, stop reading. Go rent it.) This is a powerful movie based on the true story of a man and his son. In 117 minutes, Will Smith's character goes from working family man to homeless, single dad to unpaid apprentice to successful Chicago businessman.

What about *Apollo 13* or any of the *Rocky* movies? How about Reese Witherspoon in *Legally Blonde*? The movie is a little silly, but motivating. The point is that the movies that make your heart feel stronger and motivate and enthuse you have one thing in common: Passion. So where does this passion come from? Most of the movies we rely on to motivate us are based on real-life people and their stories. That means passion comes from people. It comes from real life. Some people are born with it. Some people learn it at an early age. Movies are just movies, but having someone in your life willing to stand beside you and teach you passion by example is worth so much. This person is your cheerleader, the one who sincerely is rooting for your success. The person you can trust with your hopes and dreams. If you have had someone in your life like that, then passion is a way of life. It's something you're familiar with. Your dream is attainable because you have seen passion and know what it looks like. That generally means there was or is a person in your life who lives passionately.

When I think about overcoming the odds and rising above life's hardships, one particular woman comes to mind. She's worked extremely hard all her life. She raised four sons in dangerous and violent, crime-ridden neighborhoods with very limited financial resources. She made those four children her most important priority in life; to nurture them, care for them, and make sure they were safe. She was tough and strong and never gave up and no matter what happened in her life, she put those children front and center. She believed in a lot of things, among them, respect, self-respect and family. She put her sons before herself. She is the type of person you learn from with just observing. Growing up, I watched this woman and learned by her example. She's taught me a lot of things.

"With nothing, I did the best I could," she said. "Even though it's difficult to be poor, I was strong."

WHAT'S NEXT FOR YOU?

This woman stood up to anyone who got in the way of the safety of her family. This woman taught me to stick to anything and everything I put my mind to. She taught me to never give up.

"I raised my sons," she said. "I lashed out at life and the world, without much education, without guidance, or being forewarned on what lied ahead. I walked through very dark roads."

I know this woman very well and she recently shared with me that her sons meant the world to her. She said it meant everything to see them laugh and be successful. She celebrated their victories, no matter how small. She watched their progress and she still does today. She's a very intelligent woman full of real life experience. When I asked her "What do you think influences children the most?" she said, "There are so many things that are bad and good influences so that's why the absence of a father has an adverse effect. There are so many things that can influence us, especially children in society that if appointed I could write my own book. I don't think it would have an end, especially in these times- to see violence not only in society but also in the home. Do you know that I've even come to think that we parents can innocently influence a child…that many times we are living very difficult stages in life and although you may want to influence in the best way possible, there will be an imperfection in every human being that will cause us to fail and without noticing, we become a bad influence, especially when parents are separated."

Wow.

She says she has big dreams, and the biggest one is seeing her children's dreams become true. She said "being a mother for me is also a success, because I get to see successes achieved in the ones that I have raised, my sons." That's very powerful. That's what passion will do.

Sometimes family members are our best sources of inspiration. Abraham Lincoln credited his mother for his strong morals and motivation when he said, "All that I am or hope to be, I owe to my mother."

How many of us can say that?

There are so many influences in a child's life, both good and bad. As a father, I am very aware of how difficult life can be and how hard it is to raise responsible, happy, motivated, and successful children. Despite the numerous hardships, though, Abe Lincoln's mother did it…and my own mother did it, too.

My mother is very happy for me. She is happy to see the success I have worked toward and achieved in my life. She says that makes her a success. She feels talented and happy because of my life's achievements. That's because my mother worked hard to achieve her dream too. A loving and nurturing home was the most important thing to her. So was instilling the best values in us and she worked tirelessly to make that happen. I learned from her. One of the values that I learned from my mother was respect. She taught us to respect other people, but more importantly, she taught us to respect ourselves.

When we are kids, we learn to respect our parents, our teachers, our elders and the people in our communities who keep us safe. We learn to respect rules at home and at school. We learn to respect other people's feelings, their family traditions, cultural differences and opinions, but learning to respect ourselves is just as important, according to my mom. Respecting yourself means valuing who you are as a person. Confucius (551-479 BC), the Chinese teacher and philosopher, said that if you respect yourself, others will respect you.

Think about that for a moment.

If living your dream means owning your own business, part of your success will depend on whether or not your employees and customers respect you. I was lucky. I learned the meaning of respect from my mom. You have to strengthen your self-respect in order to be successful. I worked hard because I knew that being a good employee is a good way to learn to be a good employer. It's kind of like that saying about how you can't really love another person unless you love yourself. It's the same for respect. It is next to impossible to respect other people unless you respect yourself first.

That boss who was unreasonable or irrational probably didn't have a whole lot of self-respect. I'm not making excuses for behavior that is unacceptable, I'm just saying that every situation is an opportunity to learn something new…and every time you do that, you are building up an account of experiences that will help you when it is time to live your dream.

WHAT'S NEXT FOR YOU?

I have a large storehouse of positive values and experiences thanks to my mother. Through her struggles and life experiences, she taught me to respect myself and never give up on me or my dream. She's shared with me that she used to think about being successful and that she thought that the person who was successful was the one who studied; the one who graduated to become someone important and is rich and has high triumphs. "That's what I thought," she said. "Raising children also makes you a success" she says and I agree.

Thanks, Mom!

Mothers…

Throughout history, mothers have had a big influence on their children. Here are a few examples of what some successful people feel about their mother's influence.

"To describe my mother would be to write about a hurricane in its perfect power." –*Maya Angelou, poet, educator, civil rights activist.*

"Men are what their mothers made them." - *Ralph Waldo Emerson (1803-1882), American essayist, poet, lecturer.*

"My mom had a real calm about her. She was a charming woman. She wasn't an advice giver. She was just a teacher." - *Martha Stewart, business woman, magazine publisher, author, television personality*

"My mother was the independent one, and had the spirit that allowed me to be an entrepreneur…when no one else believed, she believed." - *Russell Simmons, founder of Def Jam Records and Rush Communications, Inc.*

Take a few minutes and think about your childhood, your mother or father, or a person who influenced your life. If you can't think of one person who made a difference, maybe there was an event or turning point. Close your eyes and think about that person or event. Picture something in your mind that brings it all back. Now spend a few minutes writing about it.

_____

_____

_____

_____

That memory of the person or time in your life was one of many people and events that built your character. Things like that are plentiful in all of our lives. We use them as life lessons, learn from them and move on. The point is, sometimes we have to look back, even if it's just for a short while, in order to get motivated to move forward. These snapshots of our past lives help strengthen us, help us to believe in ourselves and make us unstoppable.

American architect, writer, and educator Frank Lloyd Wright (1867-1959) once said, "The thing always happens that you really believe in; and the belief in a thing makes it happen." In other words, believing in yourself creates an environment for success. I believed in myself and am now living my dream. How about you? Are you unstoppable?

Now this may sound a lot like not giving up, but being unstoppable is very different. Dictionary.com defines unstoppable as not capable of being stopped, unbeatable, and extremely forceful. With your dream at stake, unstoppable is a good quality to have. My mother was unstoppable and now, so am I.

So if you need a little inspiration, a little push, here's a little something fun.

Remember what I said at the beginning of this chapter about how motivational movies inspire us to leap over our obstacles, meet our challenges and courageously go after our goals? Well, according to the Internet Movie Database (IMDb), here are the top ten motivational movies of all time. If you haven't seen the movie, go rent it.

1. *A Beautiful Mind* (2001)
2. *Casablanca* (1942)

WHAT'S NEXT FOR YOU?

3. *The Grapes of Wrath* (1940)
4. *Dead Poets Society* (1989)
5. *Shane* (1953)
6. *12 Angry Men* (1957)
7. *Rocky* (1976)
8. *Life is Beautiful* (1997)
9. *Taste of Cherry* (1997)
10. *Cool Hand Luke* (1967)

Other motivational movies include *Freedom Writers* (2007), *Erin Brockovich* (2000), *The Blind Side* (2009) and *Never Been Kissed* (1999).

Now back to the woman I described earlier in this chapter. You remember. She was the one who never gave up and took pride in the way she raised her children. That was her dream- to raise four young boys safely into adulthood. Well, if you haven't already figured it out, that strong woman is my mother. She taught me to never give up…and even though it took me six years to achieve my dream, I'm here because I never gave up. I dove in and chased my dream passionately to its fulfillment.

Dig deep. You are reading this book. You haven't given up on your dream. I know you have what it takes. Wherever and whoever helped you get to where you are now, whether you remember the experiences to be good or bad, it doesn't matter anymore. This is where you are now. There's only one person in the world that needs to be content with the position you are in, and that's you. I grew up in a home where giving up was not an option and as the result of watching a woman who doesn't care about success, I learned how to succeed.

Chapter Seventeen
THE EQUATION FOR SUCCESS

"The question isn't who is going to let me; it's who is going to stop me."
-Ayn Rand, Novelist, Philosopher

At the beginning of the second part of this book, I said that everyone is allowed to participate and contribute. We all hold a ticket to what's out there in the world around us...and that means you, too. You have the potential to play in the same playground as the thinkers, creators, teachers and entrepreneurs of our world. Hopefully by now you believe that...and know that you can be someone who can make a difference; you believe that you are someone who can live your dream.

So many people walk around this life just surviving; waking up, dragging themselves out of bed. Working at a job they do not enjoy or that doesn't challenge them. This is not the career path they love. This is a job they show up to everyday because they have to pay the mortgage or the car payment or the bills. This is not their dream.

But this is not you.

You have a dream and are willing to do whatever it takes to get there. You are almost finished reading this book. You have asked yourself countless times, "What's next for me?" You are reading and learning and talking about your dream to supportive people who are encouraging you to live the life you want. It feels great, doesn't it? You know what you want to do and have been gathering and using the tools to go out and pursue it. You are ready to use what you learned to chase your dream and live the life you want to live, but before I let you go, there is one more important thing I want to share with you: My equation for success.

> **PASSION + DEDICATION + TIME = SUCCESS**

Throughout this book, I have preached all three parts of this equation. Choosing a dream means finding something you are so passionate about that you are willing to invest the time it takes to make it happen. The passion part is the dream…and it's the passion that ignites the desire, the motivation and the energy you'll need to want to invest the time necessary to achieve success.

> **"The passion part is the dream…and it's the passion that ignites the desire, the motivation and the energy you'll need to want to invest the time necessary to achieve success."**

Think of passion as a wildfire.

Once a wildfire gets going, it can burn out of control and create a lot of damage. Many things can get a wildfire started, but only one thing can stop it: Perseverance. Firefighters must relentlessly and aggressively fight the fire with water until it is under control. This is because they know that if they do not get it under control, it will cause damage that may take years and years to recover from. So, if your passion is like a wildfire, getting it focused and under control so that you can use it to achieve your dream is like what firefighters do. They stay with it. They put in the time. They are prepared and ready and know exactly what they are doing.

This is what you have to do, too.

Fernando's Equation for Success:

PASSION + DEDICATION + TIME = SUCCESS

SUCCESS: Success is the end result of this equation. It's your vision for the future. It's where you want to go and be. To look at the big picture and work backwards means starting with how you want your life to look. So…how do you want your life to look?

_____

_____

_____

_____

PASSION: This is where it all starts. This is your dream plus how you feel about your dream. What is your passion?

_____

_____

_____

_____

DEDICATION: This is where the worksheets and time management tools come into play. This is the part where no matter how many challenges get in

WHAT'S NEXT FOR YOU?

the way, you find a way to leap over them. You are fueled by your passion and as a result, are focused on crossing the finish line. What does dedication mean to you? How will you use what you've read about in this book to move your life forward?

_____

_____

_____

_____

TIME: Putting the time in goes without saying. Everything and anything worth doing requires an investment of time. That's it. It's hard work. It's not easy. But if you are willing to put the time in, the rewards will be great. You will be living your dream and what is better than that?

I never once said this process would be easy, but I will say that this simple formula worked for me. Everyone has challenges. Overcome them. Everyone has a dream. Chase yours.

There once was a young boy. As he sat in one of his Bronx, NY, junior high school classes, his teacher asked, "What do you want to be when you grow up?" Without even blinking, this boy threw his hand up and said, "a millionaire."

This surprised the teacher and he asked the boy how he was planning to do that. The boy thought for a moment and said that he wanted to become a millionaire working at an honest business that he knew and even at a young age, he knew exactly what that was. A born entrepreneur, this boy sold handmade ties and fashionable suits to his classmates in high school. After he graduated, he started working as a stock boy. Then he studied business for two years at Baruch College, dropped out, and enlisted in the United States Army. He served in the army from 1962 to 1964. As soon as he was home, this young man began working as a salesman for Brooks Brothers, the New York City-based high-end clothing store, but his dream was to someday work for himself, like me. After earning some money from a clothing manufacturer in Manhattan who was impressed by his designs, this young man started his own business: a necktie store. He created and manufactured his own neckties under the label "Polo."

In New York City, people began to notice these unique and well-made ties. Many men began coming to the store and buying them. The more popular this young man's ties became, the more determined he was to continue pursuing his dream of becoming a millionaire. Then, in 1976, with an investment of $50,000, he started his own company and called it Polo. He began designing more than neckties. He made fine men's clothing and eventually created a line for women. According to Forbes magazine, in March 2012, this man's net worth was about $7.5 billion.

Born Ralph Lipschitz to a Bronx homemaker and a house painter, he knew exactly what his dream was at a very young age. He stayed focused on what he wanted and made it his life. Designing ties and clothes was something he loved. It was something he was passionate about. He took that love of creating fine clothing and dedicated all of his time to it. He was dedicated and passionate and knew that in order to achieve millionaire status – which was his dream – he would have to invest his time and life into it.

And he did.

And look what happened.

This man is Ralph Lauren, and there's a lot to be learned from people like him.

Now. Let's take the Ralph Lauren story and apply it to my simple equation for success. To Ralph Lauren, SUCCESS meant someday becoming a millionaire. He took his PASSION for designing neckties and clothing and started small. He worked hard and showed DEDICATION to his passion by focusing and never getting too far from his dream. He put in hours and hours of TIME, designing, creating, marketing, learning, and working on his ideas. His life revolved around getting to where he wanted to be. Ralph Lauren took his passion and dedication, added his time and it equaled success for him. [47]

The great thing about my equation for success is that it can be duplicated and adapted to fit any scenario, any dream, any life. Designing fashion is not my thing. I am not passionate about neckties. I could try to use the equation to open a men's clothing store, but it wouldn't work for me. What worked for Ralph Lauren is not going to work for anyone else in the same way. My dream was to own a business. I was passionate about my dream. I was dedicated to getting there and invested the time. I now own my business and am a success.

Bottom line: Choose one thing you are passionate about. Chase it. Add dedication and time and you WILL be a success.

I can't end this book without a few words about quality of life. Everything I've shared with you is true and like I said just a few pages back, I never once said this would be easy. It's a process that will take motivation, determination and dedication. It will cut into your social life and make you obsess over things you never thought you'd obsess over. But I promise it will all be worth it in the end.

You may feel afraid, but stare your fear in the face. Spend some time soul searching and thinking about what fears might be holding you back. Ask yourself why you are afraid and then answer honestly. Do not be afraid to chase who you desire to be or do. The world is constantly evolving. Be a part of that by never putting your aspirations on the back burner.

Love who you are now. Be confident and strong and people will see a leader. Appreciate your strengths and your gifts. Respect your talents. Capitalize on these. At the same time, be aware of your weaknesses. Work on them. You can do this.

Always remember that failure is really not personal. It might be about a choice you made or something you did or didn't do, but in the end, it's not about you. Everyone fails. The important thing to remember is that falling down is one thing, but picking yourself up and trying again is another and as long as you keep getting up, you are not failing.

Think good thoughts. Always.

Thank everyone who has helped you along the way. Being thankful will make you appreciate others and will make you happy. Do it. It works.

Gather as much as you can along the way to fill your warehouse with as many tools and supplies as you can. There is a child's story about a little mouse who didn't want to help all the other mice get ready for the long, cold winter.

He laid in the sun and ate lots of good things while the others gathered wheat and nuts and berries. The winter came and the mice huddled in their warm nest. Months passed and they ate and ate until all of their food was gone and when that happened, they all turned to the little mouse who did nothing to help and asked him what he had to offer. His answer was simple. He had songs and pictures in his head of warm summer days. He shared poems and described green, lush landscapes. He satisfied a part of the other mice's hunger that no one else had thought of. He took everyone's minds off the cold, gray days and the seemingly endless winter.

Be both the hard-working mice and the mouse who saw the beauty of life and was able to share it. Both camps are important in life. As you pursue your dream and build your new life, never forget how important beauty and kindness and compassion and love is.

Fill your warehouse with everything you need to succeed at your new life, and don't forget to store the warm and sunny days to pull out when you need them.

Ever read or hear about the starfish story? It goes like this.

Once there was an old man walking on a beautiful beach. The sun was setting and the waves were crashing rhythmically. He was thinking about his life and enjoying the warm breeze and the sounds and smells of the beach. Looking off into the distance, he sees someone picking something up off the sand and throwing it back into the water. The older man is curious. As he walks closer, he sees that it is a young man. The young man looks around on the sand, picks something up, and throws it back into the ocean. He does this again and again and again. The old man gets close to the young man and decides to ask him what he is doing.

"Hello," he says. "What are you doing?"

The young man stops for a moment and says, "Why, I am picking up these starfish and throwing them back into the ocean."

The old man looked around and smiled. "But why?"

"Well, the tide is going out," said the young man. "And if I don't throw them back into the water, they will die."

WHAT'S NEXT FOR YOU?

To this, the old man smiled again. He held his arms out wide and said, "Young man, there are miles and miles of beach. There are starfish scattered across the sand along every mile. You can not possibly make a difference."

The young man listened politely to what the older man had to say. Then he picked up another starfish and carefully threw it out past the breaking waves.

"I made a difference to this one," he said.

I hope I have made a difference in your life. My struggles, my pain, my passion, my hard work and my success is my life. I truly want you to achieve your dreams and live the life that you want to live, because I believe that it is in the pursuit of your dream that the most happiest days of your life exist.

So, what's next for you?

Chapter Eighteen
THE FREQUENTLY ASKED QUESTIONS CHAPTER

"The art and science of asking questions
is the source of all knowledge."
- THOMAS BERGER, AMERICAN AUTHOR

Okay, this is it. This is the Frequently Asked Questions chapter. The place where I answer questions that have been raised throughout the book so that you can have a review of the basic concepts of what I believe are the steps you need to take to go after and eventually realize your dreams. These are the answers to questions that will take you to the life you want to live, but remember…these are just a review of what you've already read in this book. Sometimes it helps to go back and reread or redo an exercise.

Q: Could I really live my dream?

A: Absolutely. By dumping all of your thoughts and energy into chasing your dream, you can definitely live the life you want. I did it. I focused on exactly what I wanted to do. I spent time each day doing that. I made it my priority and as a result, I'm living my dream.

Q: What exactly is drive?

A: In the first chapter, I wrote that what I lacked in formal education, I made up in drive. Drive is defined as striving with determination toward a goal. My drive made the world around me my classroom. I learned how to be a better employee by listening and working hard at the job I was in at the time. I asked lots of questions. I listened closely to the answers. I applied this philosophy to the material I was reading as well. The more I delved in, the more I found myself trying to create more time to invest in my dream. Drive is getting behind the wheel and stepping on the gas.

Q: How can I put more into my life to get more out?

A: That's a no-brainer. Anytime you devote more of yourself, more of your resources, more of your time and energy, your life will improve. As you hurl yourself toward the life you want to live, putting more in will always go a long way. For example, I knew while I was an employee how much I wanted to be self-employed. As a result, I created a way to find time to achieve that dream. I put more focus and motivation into the short amounts of extra time I could find in my already busy days to learn and grow. The more I learned and grew, the more I wanted to learn and grow. It became an obsession of sorts and while the word obsession is often associated with things that are not good for us, my obsession with reading, listening and learning more was a great thing. Being a little obsessed with doing what you need to do to get where you want to be is what works. Really.

Q: What did you mean when you said that your dream is like a battery?

A: Going back to my car analogy, the battery is the life of the car. Without it, the car goes nowhere. There are no lights. The windows do not move. Nothing can run without the battery. Well, without your dream to fuel your motivation, nothing will happen. That's because choosing to chase after your dream and live the life you want to live takes many, many hours of dedicated time and hard work. This is one of those times when the saying "No one ever said this would be easy" truly applies. Your dream is what fuels you. It pushes you. It propels you. Like the battery in your car, your dream is the lifeblood of your quest.

Q: Who inspired you the most?

A: Without hesitation, I can honestly say that I have been inspired the most by Napoleon Hill. Now this is not to say that many other business leaders, entrepreneurs, community leaders, or family members have not been an inspiration to me, it's just that Hill's writings have touched me. His formula for success makes sense to me. I followed it and succeeded. I attribute my success, passion, drive and desire to Napoleon Hill. I read his work and began to truly believe in myself and when I started to believe in myself, I transformed my life. There's a BIG difference between you thinking you may not be able to achieve something versus you actually accepting and believing that you can't. Remember what Napoleon Hill said, "Dreams are the cornerstone of success."

Q: Besides reading what successful people have written, what are some other ways I can fuel my dream?

A: There are so many things you can do to fuel your dream. Many of these suggestions can be done while driving to work, while at work, or during short intervals of time throughout the day. Besides sitting down and reading about how other successful people got to where they want to be, you can listen to what they wrote while driving in your car or while at work (if you are permitted to do so). You can talk to a good friend about your dream. You can visualize yourself living your dream. You can write your dream on a post-it note and stick it where you can see it. You can watch movies or listen to music that motivates you. All of these things are important because it helps you to push forward. You have to stay motivated to keep going.

Q: How do I know if I am ready to start chasing my dream?

A: Are you excited and motivated? How's your attitude? Are you serious about your success and truly focused on what you want in life? If you are all of those things, and assuming you have already identified your dream, then you are ready- ready to be focused, obsessed, brave, and relentless. If you know what you want and are willing to make the sacrifices to get there, then you are ready.

Q: I know I'm ready, so what now?

A: The first thing you need to do is organize your time and life. Complete the personal timesheets for 14 days and evaluate where you can work on your dream. Go back through this book and fill in the exercises if you haven't already done that. Make a plan. Stick to it. Tell yourself what you're going to do with your time. Plan how you will invest every hour of your days. You're either working toward something or drifting away from it. Things take time. Jump on the train to success now and allow time to work in your favor.

Twenty hours per week wasted today equates to 5,200 hours wasted in 5 years, which is 217 days of your life that could've been used to achieve your dream. Put your time into productive use. You need to manage your time efficiently and effectively today to make room for success tomorrow. This may be one of the most important things you do in your entire life.

Q: Remind me…what are the five basic and simple steps to success?
1. Have a dream
2. Focus all attention on your dream
3. Stay away from naysayers
4. Stick with it
5. A great attitude

Q: Why is it so important to ignore the naysayers?

A: Naysayers will derail, deter, and disengage you. They will sabotage your progress. You are in the middle of the fight of your life. You are juggling family responsibilities, a job, and time constraints. The very last thing you need is friends, family members, or coworkers telling you that your dream is a waste of time. Or that you will never be self-employed, own a restaurant, be a ballet dancer, cut hair professionally, ice skate in the Olympics, run for office or fly an airplane. Whatever your dream, you cannot allow negative people with pessimistic viewpoints and bad attitudes temper the way you see your success in the world. Naysayers have the potential to make you feel less than who you are. The best thing to do when someone is trying to sabotage your efforts is tell them what they are doing and ask them to stop. Be prepared to walk away from that person if you need to.

Q: What are the four truths you learned by reading and listening and living?

A: The first thing I learned is that not chasing your dream will diminish who you are. Then, the second truth is that people who follow their dreams are creators. Thirdly, I learned that pursuing my dream empowered me and made me stronger. Finally, chasing my dream educated me. Other truths I learned along the way: I'm the only one in control of my future and chasing my dream made me a better, smarter person. Hey, if living your dream was easy, everyone would be doing it. Another important point is that chasing your dream will make you happy.

Q: But what if I fail?

A: If you fail or experience a setback, who cares? Right? Do you really think that there are setback free lives? Errors and learning curves are a part of life, so accept and learn from them and just move on. Get back up and get back on track. To do that, you must believe in yourself, be positive, review the key concepts in this book and take a step forward…and then another, followed by another. You can do this!

Q: What's passion got to do with it?

A: Everything. Passion is jumping out of bed in the morning and racing out the door to live the life you just can't imagine not living. It's leaping up and living your dream because it's what will make you happy. We've talked about a lot of things in this book: dreams, motivation, time management, honesty, inspiration, drive, and car batteries and all of those things are vital to achieving your dream and the life you want to live, but without passion…well, there

WHAT'S NEXT FOR YOU?

is no greatness. If you've gotten this far and have a dream and a plan, then you have passion.

**Q: So, now it's my turn to ask: WHAT'S NEXT FOR YOU?
GO OUT AND MAKE YOUR DREAMS COME TRUE!**

APPENDIX A

Cool Stuff to Read
(in no particular order)

Hill, Napoleon. *Think and Grow Rich.* Fawcett Books, New York. May 12, 1987.

Hill, Napoleon. *The Law of Success in Sixteen Lessons.* Tribeca Books, New York, 1928.

Mycoskie, Blake. *Start Something That Matters.* Random House, Inc., New York, 2011.

Schultz, Howard. *Pour Your Heart Into It.* Hyperion, New York, 1997.

Emmert, JM. "Rich Man, Poor Man: The Story of Napoleon Hill." *Success,* http://www.success.com/articles/515-rich-man-poor-man

Comaford-Lynch, Christine. *Rules for Renegades.* McGraw-Hill, New York, 2007.

Tolkien, J.R.R. *The Lord of the Rings.* Houghton Mifflin Harcourt, Aug. 14, 2012.

WHAT'S NEXT FOR YOU?

Kiyosaki, Robert T. *Unfair Advantage: The Power of Financial Education.* Plata Publishing, 2011.

Clason, George S. *The Richest Man in Babylon.* Myriad World Publishers, 2011.

Getty, J. Paul. *How to Be Rich.* Jove, 1986.

Getty, J. Paul. *As I See It: The Autobiography of J. Paul Getty.* J. Paul Getty Museum, 2003.

Robbins, Anthony. *Awaken the Giant Within: How to Take Immediate Control of Your Mental, Emotional, Physical and Financial Destiny!* Free Press, a division of Simon & Schuster, Inc., New York, 1991.

Robbins, Anthony. *Unlimited Power: The New Science of Personal Achievement.* Free Press, a division of Simon & Schuster, Inc., New York, 1986.

Walton, Sam and John Huey. *Sam Walton: Made in America.* Bantam, 1993.

Branson, Richard. *Losing My Virginity: How I Survived, Had Fun, and Made a Fortune Doing Business My Way.* Crown Publishing Group, a Division of Random House, New York, 2002.

Branson, Richard. *Like a Virgin: Secrets They Won't Teach You at Business School.* Penguin Group, New York, 2012.

Maxwell, John C. *The 15 Invaluable Laws of Growth: Live Them and Reach Your Potential.* Hachette Book Group, New York, 2012.

Maxwell, John C. *The 21 Irrefutable Laws of Leadership: Follow Them and People Will Follow You.* Thomas Nelson, Inc., Nashville, TN, 1998 and 2007.

Maxwell, John C. *The 5 Levels of Leadership: Proven Steps to Maximize Your Potential.* Hachette Book Group, New York, 2011.

Conwell, Russell H. *Acres of Diamonds.* CreateSpace Independent Publishing Platform, 2011.

Ziglar, Zig. *Secrets of Closing the Sale.* Fleming H. Revell, a division of Baker Publishing Group, Grand Rapids, MI, 2003.

Ziglar, Zig. *Better Than Good: Creating a Life You Can't Wait to Live.* Thomas Nelson, Inc., Nashville, TN, 2006

APPENDIX B

Name:		Date:	
	Personal Timesheet		
12:00 AM			
12:30 AM			
1:00 AM			
1:30 AM			
2:00 AM			
2:30 AM			
3:00 AM			
3:30 AM			
4:00 AM			
4:30 AM			
5:00 AM			
5:30 AM			
6:00 AM			
6:30 AM			
7:00 AM			
7:30 AM			
8:00 AM			
8:30 AM			
9:00 AM			
9:30 AM			
10:00 AM			
10:30 AM			
11:00 AM			
11:30 AM			
12:00 PM			
12:30 PM			
1:00 PM			
1:30 PM			
2:00 PM			
2:30 PM			
3:00 PM			
3:30 PM			
4:00 PM			
4:30 PM			
5:00 PM		8:30 PM	
5:30 PM		9:00 PM	
6:00 PM		9:30 PM	
6:30 PM		10:00 PM	
7:00 PM		10:30 PM	
7:30 PM		11:00 PM	
8:00 PM		11:30 PM	

SUMMARY BOX

Category	Hours

WHAT'S NEXT FOR YOU?

Daily Worksheet

Date:

High Priority (20%/80% Results)	Business Tasks
1	1
2	2
3	3
4	4
5	5
6	6
7	7
8	8
9	9
10	10
Personal Tasks	11
1	12
2	13
3	14
4	15

Appointments

5:30 AM	2:00 PM
6:00 AM	2:30 PM
6:30 AM	3:00 PM
7:00 AM	3:30 PM
7:30 AM	4:00 PM
8:00 AM	4:30 PM
8:30 AM	5:00 PM
9:00 AM	5:30 PM
9:30 AM	6:00 PM
10:00 AM	6:30 PM
10:30 AM	7:00 PM
11:00 AM	7:30 PM
11:30 AM	8:00 PM
12:00 PM	8:30 PM
12:30 PM	9:00 PM
1:00 PM	9:30 PM
1:30 PM	10:00 PM

Messaging & Notes

ENDNOTES

[1] Hill, Napoleon (1937). *Think and Grow Rich,* Chicago, Illinois: Combined Registry Company. p. 14.

[2] Walmart.com, Retrieved from http://corporate.walmart.com/our-story/heritage/sam-walton

[3] The Napoleon Hill Foundation, Retrieved from http://www.naphill.org/about-napoleon-hill/ and http://www.naphill.org/about-napoleon-hill/andrew-carnegie-biography/

[4] "John Maxwell: Attitude is the Difference Maker," Retrieved from http://www.success.com/articles/1056-maxwell-attitude-is-the-difference-maker

[5] "America's Beloved Best Friend." Academy of Achievement, Nov. 28, 2011. Retrieved from http://www.achievement.org/autodoc/page/win0bio-1 and "Oprah Winfrey's Official Biography." Oprah.com, Retrieved from http://www.oprah.com/pressroom/Oprah-Winfreys-Official-Biography

[6] http://www.monticello.org/site/jefferson/nothing-can-stop-man-right-mental-attitude-quotation

WHAT'S NEXT FOR YOU?

[7] "Robert Edward (Ted) Turner." Academy of Achievement, Nov. 20, 2007. Retrieved from http://www.achievement.org/autodoc/page/tur0bio-1

[8] http://www.the-benefits-of-positive-thinking.com/attitude-quotes.html

[9] "Mickey Mantle Stats." Baseball Almanac. Retrieved from http://www.baseball-almanac.com/players/player.php?p=mantlmi01

[10] http://www.usatoday.com/news/nation/story/2011-12-27/most-admired-people-2011/52243574/1

[11] Hill, Napoleon. *Think and Grow Rich*. Fawcett Books, New York. May 12, 1987.

[12] Pells, Eddie, "Snowboarder who nearly died returns to slopes for first time." NBC NEWS.com, Dec. 14, 2011. Retrieved from http://today.msnbc.msn.com/id/45668109/ns/today-good_news/t/snowboarder-who-nearly-died-returns-slopes-first-time/#

[13] "Featured Quotes," Vince Lombardi.com. Retrieved from http://www.vincelombardi.com/quotes.html

[14] McLeon, S.A. (2007). *Maslow's Hierachy of Needs*. Retrieved from http://www.simplypsychology.org/maslow.html

[15] Mycoskie, Blake. *Start Something That Matters*. Random House, Inc., New York, 2011.

[16] About Blake, startsomethingthatmatters.com. Retrieved from http://www.startsomethingthatmatters.com/about-blake/.

[17] "Mary Kay Ash: Remembering Her Life," Her Life, marykaytribute.com. Retrieved from http://www.marykaytribute.com/HerLife.aspx

[18] "Parents Influence Children's Success, Duke Social Psychologist Says." Duke Today, Aug. 14, 2004. Retrieved from http://today.duke.edu/2004/08/success_0804.html

[19] Mary Kay.com. Retrieved from http://www.marykay.com.ph/mkpweb08/company/Founder.asp

[20] Hill, Napoleon. *The Law of Success in Sixteen Lessons.* Tribeca Books, New York, 1928.

[21] Schultz, Howard. *Pour Your Heart Into It.* Hyperion, New York, 1997.

[22] http://www.starbucks.com/about-us/company-information

[23] "Jim Rohn's Biography," Jimrohn.com. Retrieved from http://www.jimrohn.com/index.php?main_page=page&id=1177

[24] http://earlshoaff.info/

[25] Rohn, Jim. *The Five Major Pieces to the Life Puzzle.* Jim Rohn International, February 1991.

[26] Ankeny, Jason. "Mike Wolfe of 'American Pickers' is the New Americana Idol." *Entrepeneur*, August 31, 2011. Retrieved from http://www.entrepreneur.com/article/220176

[27] Comaford-Lynch, Christine. *Rules for Renegades.* McGraw-Hill, New York, 2007.

[28] Tolkien, J.R.R. *The Lord of the Rings.* Houghton Mifflin Harcourt, Aug. 14, 2012.

[29] www.weightwatchters.com

WHAT'S NEXT FOR YOU?

[30] "Pareto principle." BusinessDictionary.com. Retrieved from http://www.businessdictionary.com/definition/Pareto-principle.html

[31] Mount, Ian. "David Neeleman, JetBlue." *Inc. Magazine,* Mansueto Ventures LLC, Retrieved from http://www.inc.com/magazine/20040401/25neeleman.html

[32] "10 Business Blunders." Virgin Media.com, Retrieved from http://www.virginmedia.com/money/features/business-blunders.php?ssid=3

[33] "Frederick W. Smith," Academy of Achievement, Jan. 9, 2008. Retrieved from http://www.achievement.org/autodoc/page/smi0bio-1

[34] "About Mrs. Fields." DebbiFields.com. Retrieved from http://debbifields.com/about.html

[35] Ibid.

[36] "Chester F. Carlson." Britannica. Retrieved from http://www.britannica.com/EBchecked/topic/96110/Chester-F-Carlson

[37] http://www.leedeforest.org/Home.html

[38] "Traveling Through Time." NOVA Online, November 2000. Retrieved from http://www.pbs.org/wgbh/nova/time/through2.html

[39] http://allaboutstevejobs.com/

[40] "Henry Ford, Biography." Bio.com. Retrieved from http://www.biography.com/people/henry-ford-9298747

[41] http://www.jgrisham.com/bio/

[42] "Sam Walton." Walmart.com. Retrieved from http://corporate.walmart.com/our-story/heritage/sam-walton

[43] Ibid.

[44] "Napoleon Hill." Retrieved from http://napoleonhill.wwwhubs.com/

[45] "Sam Walton." Walmart.com. Retrieved from http://corporate.walmart.com/our-story/heritage/sam-walton

[46] "Kathryn Joosten: Biography." Retrieved from http://www.kathrynjoosten.com/biography.shtml

[47] "Ralph Lauren Biography." *Encyclopedia of World Biography.* Retrieved from http://www.notablebiographies.com/Ki-Lo/Lauren-Ralph.html#b

What's Your Story?

www.fatepublishing.com
support@fatepublishing.com

OUR MISSION IS TO HELP YOU TELL YOUR STORY

www.ingramcontent.com/pod-product-compliance
Lightning Source LLC
Chambersburg PA
CBHW061653040426
42446CB00010B/1721